FINANCIAL COACH
SHANNAAN DAWDA

FROM
PAYCHECKS TO
POWER

7

POWER
MOVES
TO UNLOCK
WEALTH
BUILDING

From Paychecks to Power

7 Power Moves to Unlock Wealth Building by Shannaan Dawada

True Financial
http://www.truefinancialcoaches.com
http://www.FromPaycheckstoPower.com

Unattributed quotations are by Shannaan Dawda

ISBN: 978-0-9961303-0-1

Manufactured in the United States of America

For wholesale pricing, event bookings, and all other inquiries email: Go to www.FromPaychecksToPower.com

Table of Contents

INTRODUCTION:
In the Wealthiest Nation in the World, Why Are We SO Darn Broke?

CHAPTER 1: A Journey to Broke and Back: My Story
CHAPTER 2: It's Called "Personal Finance" for a Reason!
CHAPTER 3: Who Are You When It Comes to Managing Money?
CHAPTER 4: What's Your "Why"?
CHAPTER 5: What's Your Financial Kryptonite?
CHAPTER 6: The Credit Score Myth – EXPOSED!
CHAPTER 7: The Final Step before the Official Journey: Detoxing with a Financial Fast!

Power Move 1: Plan, then Command Your Money!
Power Move 2: Get Your Snowball on a Roll!
Power Move 3: Take the Urgency Out of Emergency!
Power Move 4: Invest Today for a Comfortable Tomorrow!
Power Move 5: Eliminate the Fees from Your Kids' Degrees!
Power Move 6: Make Your House a Home, Not a Prison!
Power Move 7: More Money = More Options to Give & Live!

BONUS CHAPTER: Common Personal Finance Myths – EXPOSED!

APPENDIX 1: Sample Budget
APPENDIX 2: "What's Your Financial Personality?" Assesment

What Others Are Saying...

"Thanks for your encouragement in having financial peace. My knowledge of finance has improved a great deal just by reading your blogs and participating in your fast. As of yesterday, my undergrad student loan ($5,000) has a zero balance! No more Sallie Mae for me!" - Erica, Consultant & Federal Accountant

"Today, I decided to see how much progress I've made since I started with the debt payoff plan... $9700+ in the time span of three months. I can hardly believe it! I just wanted to thank you for helping to get me on the right track and mindset with eliminating this debt and building for my future. This experience has definitely helped me look at my financial decisions in a new light. Thank you!" - Charlie, Project Coordinator

"I LOVED the book! It was an easy read, it was engaging, it was practical, and honestly, it wasn't a bore like many of the other financial books that are on the market. I also enjoyed hearing your story, and I appreciated the personal stories that you used throughout." - Dr. Shannon, President of Houston Writers Block

"I got tired of making excuses and made things happen instead. Thank you Shannaan Dawda for continuing to show others your passion about financial freedom. I am a believer because of you. Thank you for your encouragement and coaching!" - Darinee, Outreach Manager

Acknowledgments

First and foremost, I want to thank God for blessing me with this knowledge and the life journey that led me to attain an understanding of this message. It is through getting my own finances in order that I found Him, and I have been growing spiritually ever since.

I also would like to thank my parents, who have always been my number one supporters. You always told me to be great and that nothing is impossible. You are more of an inspiration to me than you know! You left all that you knew in Ghana to embark upon a great journey of unknowns, taking the first step when you didn't see the whole staircase; that is what life is all about. You have instilled valuable principles and beliefs into my life that have led me to where I am now, and for this, I am grateful.

To my sisters Khadijat and Aiesha, thank you for being such awesome siblings. I remember when we would sneak outside to go play and one of us would keep lookout for Mom or Dad's car through the woods behind the house! We ride or die for each other, and I love you both for that.

To my best friend, Michael, thanks for constantly staying on top of me as I embarked upon this journey. Thank you also for continually reminding me about the purpose for which I started financially coaching others.

Finally, to everyone else that has impacted my life, thank you. There are so many of you to thank that it would literally take a few pages to list you all. I am forever grateful for your influences in my life, and I hope to make you proud.

For Your Free Budget Form

http://www.TrueFinancialCoaches.com

Visit

www.FromPaychecksTo Power.com

For Speaking, Coaching, or Other Events Contact

INTRODUCTION
In the Wealthiest Nation in the World, Why Are We SO Darn Broke?

With as many years as I've gone to school, as many hours as I work a week, as financially responsible I am, and as many sacrifices I've made in my life for so many years trying to get ahead, why am I STILL so darn BROKE? Will things ever change for me? How will I EVER get ahead if things continue like this? If you've ever asked yourself either of these questions, or any variation of them, you are not alone! Millions of people, from twenty-somethings to sixty-somethings silently ask themselves these questions every day as they sit at their computers or tap away at their mobile phones to pay creditors, utility providers, and other debtors online. In reality, most of them earn a reasonable living wage and are paid respectable salaries. However, with each dollar that they must spend to make ends meet every month, their hopes for ever being able to build a secure financial future, drain just as rapidly as their bank accounts.

Today Americans live in what is arguably the wealthiest country in the world. However, according statistics reported by The Wall Street Journal, 70% of Americans live from paycheck to paycheck!

Why is that? In countries such as France and Germany, citizens have a savings rate five times higher than that of U.S. citizens, even though the U.S. has a stronger economy. The reason for this disparity is grounded in the fact that Americans are unknowingly being robbed of their most powerful wealth building tool: their income!

One might ask, "Robbed? How is it possible that Americans are being robbed of their income?" The answer is simple. Each time Americans give away a portion of their income in the form of "easy and convenient low monthly payments" that are offered by everyone from furniture stores to student loan providers, they are essentially being robbed by their creditors and being positioned for a lifetime of being broke. Considering this, most Americans are completely unaware that they have a series of weapons pointed at them by impatient creditors demanding, "Give me all of your money." Because, let's face it: installments are how the majority of Americans have learned to live and try to financially survive!

What's more, most Americans are never taught the proper fundamentals of personal finance, so they never actually come to the realization that they are being robbed! Instead, they just continue happily along, financing their lives away, struggling to make ends meet, and thinking that all is well, as long as they are satisfying their creditors through the submission of the "easy and convenient low monthly payment" installments that never seem to end.

I've spent years as a financial coach, working with people who, despite their education, planning, and good intentions, never seem to break out of the cycle of living from paycheck to paycheck. When they come to me, their motivation for doing so, is to break free from the pressure of being in debt and to get their finances in order, so that they can begin to either use their hard-earned monies for living the lives they have always dreamt of living and/or saving their money to secure their financial future. However, what they do not realize is that the effects of getting their finances in order are far reaching - into virtually every area of their lives. When they get their finances in order and start winning with their money, other areas of their lives also begin to prosper. As I have worked with countless clients to repair their finances, I have seen broken relationships healed, life passions re-discovered, and even the achievement of physical fitness goals! The reason for this: the vast majority of people do not realize the significant impact that their fragile and out-of-control financial states are having on their lives. While not living from paycheck to paycheck and having the ability to retire wealthy are all great objectives that you will learn from this book, my bigger objective is to help you to realize the newfound control, clarity and passion for life that you will find as a side-effect of getting your finances finally in order.

This book is designed to equip you with valuable tools and information that will empower you to achieve your financial goals. I'll bet that you are wondering, "Is this stuff really going to work?" The answer is yes! It will work, but it will also require work from you! There is nothing worth attaining in life that doesn't require you to work for it. Anything that you desire to be successful at, whether graduating from college, being physically in shape, being good at your hobby, or doing anything else worth doing, will require you to earn it.

Mind you, this book will not teach you how to engage in a one-shot deal that magically produces financial prosperity. Instead, it will teach a way of life to which you must subscribe and live by, on a daily basis; to do this, you must commit to walking the path of financial excellence. There are no hand-outs in life, so this won't come easily. I challenge you to dig deep, get your mind right, and prepare for a battle that is going to require your focus, dedication, and persistence in order for you to become victorious. If you can commit to these things, I can definitely help you win with your money!

CHAPTER 1
A Journey to Broke and Back: My Story

Growing up, I learned a lot about personal finances from my parents; I received an up-close-and-personal education from them on how to handle money. However, here's the thing about the education we receive from our parents: because they serve as our primary instructors during the most developmental years of our lives, what they teach us out of their experiences tend to become our own experiences – good or bad. Thus, most people will most likely end up living out the same philosophies, principles, and practices to which they were exposed by their parents. If the lessons they have taught us are good, when we embrace and live according to them, we fare well. On the flip side, if the lessons that they have taught us are not so good, when we embrace and live according to them, we come up empty and lacking.

What I did not know during the time that I was growing up and absorbing lessons about personal financial management from my parents is that rather than teaching me what I should do to prosper financially, they were expert instructors at what not to do! Mind you, I love my parents dearly; they are the most important people in the world to me, and I value all that they have tried to do for me and all of the guidance that they provided for me in life. Thus, I do not disparage them for the financial choices that they made while they were raising me; they clearly made what they thought were the best financial decisions for them and their family's future, based upon the information they had access to at the time. In fact, they are no different from you, me, or anyone else; every day, we make financial choices that are based upon the information that we have access to as a result of what we have been taught by our family members and friends and from our experiences and education. Unfortunately, much of what we have learned from our family and friends is ineffective at helping us to build the wealth we desire to have, and education systems – both public and private – tend to remain conspicuously silent when it comes to teaching people how to properly manage their finances.

To my dismay, it was only later in life that I came to the profound realization that all that I had learned through the years about financial management and wealth building needed to be un-learned if I was ever going to really get ahead with my finances. With the rich education that my journey afforded me, I learned a plethora lessons – lessons that I desire to share with as many people as possible, so that they do not find themselves replicating the same mistakes I made. Thus, I offer you the gift of my story: a series of experiences that dot my journey to being relentlessly broke and back.

My financial journey kicked off when I was 19 years old. At 19, I was working at a full-service carwash making about $250 a week. For a college student living at home with my parents at the time, that wasn't bad! No living expenses and no bills of my own, meant that I could pocket all of the money that I took home. It was nice having disposable income in my pocket, but for me, it wasn't enough. As an ambitious and progressive 19 year old, I was looking to make some big money – fast!

Unfortunately, I wanted to make my "big money" so fast that I had the unfortunate privilege of falling victim to one of those Nigerian money schemes. You know. The ones you hear about on the news when a reporter is interviewing people who are looking desperate and sheepish in front of the camera because they had to openly admit their foolishness for being so naïve. The ones at which you shake your head while you watch the victim, thinking to yourself, "How could someone be so gullible? What a sucker!" Yep... I happen to have been one of those gullible suckers.

In my case, I met the fraudster online in a chat room – yes, a chat room of all places! I know – I'm showing my age here, but it bears mentioning, because there are still those who chat through a number of internet forums. The person on the other end of the conversation made me an offer that I could not refuse. She said that she would have a $3,000 check sent to me. Once I received it, I could keep half of it, and all I had to do was send her the other half, so I did just that. Easy as pie! It was the quickest $1,500 I had ever made! Little did I know, but I would soon be in for a rude awakening.

I will never forget the moment I found out that I had been scammed. On my lunch break a few days later, I attempted to pay for a Subway sandwich, and my debit card was declined. I found this very unusual, because I knew that I had money in the bank. Sure that this was just some mix-up, I walked next door to my bank in order to inquire about what was going on with my account. It was then that the teller informed me that the check that I had deposited had been fraudulent! Even worse, I was told that I had 45 days to repay the owed balance, or else I would be reported to the FBI!

As a 19 year old, I didn't know what to do! The responsible guy that I was, nothing like this had ever happened to me before, so I was at a loss. Though I was embarrassed beyond belief for having done something so stupid, I knew that I had to tell my parents. However, as you can imagine, I was reluctant to do so because I knew how they were going to react – like typical parents would! I knew that there was going to be the initial yelling and "What the heck were you thinking boy!" So I waited a little while before I shared my big mess-up with them. I needed to get my plan together before I approached them. Once the time was right and I figured out how I was going to handle the matter, I came clean, sharing all of the details about what had occurred, with my parents. I was 100% right about their reaction! My dad launched into a lecture about how there is no such thing as getting rich quickly. My mom is pretty emotional, and in situations like these, anything she said would have just come out as a bunch of high energy yelling, so she tried not to say anything. I say "tried" because she didn't exactly succeed in her attempt. She couldn't help but interject a few of her own choice words as she listened to the conversation between my dad and me!

After my parents' initial reaction, the conclusion was clear. They explained that since I had created the mess, I needed to fix it. It helped that I had already developed a practical and realistic plan to make things right, and they were pleased to see that I was serious and mature enough to take full responsibility for what had occurred – and for dealing with it. From there, handling the matter was up to me. Needless to say, this is now a legendary story that comes up at family gatherings every year! It is a story from which I learned one of my greatest lessons about money in life: the best way to get rich quick is, DON'T!

After I had finally shared the issue with my parents, which was perhaps the greatest and most fearful obstacle of all, I was determined to get through the situation by attacking it head-on. I was making money at the carwash, so I knew that I had access to some cash – not a lot in the scope of what I needed to come up with, but it was a start. I pledged to myself to do all that I could to dig my way out of this hole that I had created for myself. It was my gullible mistake, so it was also my responsibility – no one else's.

This exercise of rescuing my finances was the first experience that I would ever have in learning the maximum effect of budgeting. Who knew that one could stretch $250 the way I did? I amazed myself with how little money I could survive on when I needed to; since I still lived at home, I spent money on gas and... well... that was about it! However, despite my best budgeting efforts, there was no way that I could pay off my negative bank balance without some assistance. Enter the hero that saved the day -- my 17 year-old sister. Though she was only working at McDonald's at the time, she gladly and willingly helped me out with the limited resources she had. When I reached day 44 of the bank's deadline and was still short some funds, she paid the remaining balance of what I lacked. Afterwards, I paid her back weekly. Though this financial fiasco had jolted me into a new reality, I was proud of myself for doing what I needed to do to get myself out of it.

The next life event that occurred on my financial journey occurred only a year later when I was 20 years old. My mother filed for bankruptcy as a result of consumer debt that consisted of primarily credit card debt. I was a student attending Georgia Southern University at the time. When she disclosed her plans to file for bankruptcy to me, I was not equipped to understand the seriousness of the decision she'd made. Yes, I had heard of the term "bankruptcy" before, but I really didn't know what it meant. The most that I could explain about it at the time was that my mother could not pay back the money that she had borrowed, and because of it, she had to go to court. I would not go on to understand the seriousness of the matter until years later, when I would eventually earn my finance degree.

I had the unfortunate displeasure of witnessing first-hand the pain and the hurt that bankruptcy brought to my parents' lives. My mom told me about how she was crying in the courtroom as she explained their financial situation to the judge. In taking on debt that she could not pay back, she felt bad. She felt like a liar. She felt like a person who was not true to her word. From my parents' experiences, I learned a lesson that would stick with me for a lifetime: going through a bankruptcy is a very traumatic occurrence that can leave one feeling like a complete and utter failure, so avoid it if at all possible.

As I spent many hours thinking about my parents' bankruptcy, I thought to myself, "How did this happen?" Years prior, they had travelled frequently, taking international trips at a rate of one every other year; frequently buying newer models of used cars with cash; and providing parts of the cash flow for my sister's and my college tuition. For all intents and purposes, my parents could have been considered "Very well off" in the financial category. However, while they might have been doing well in one season, something happened -- recession. The slowdown of the economy in 2008 had taken its toll on my parents' cash flow and reserves. Emergency funds had been completely used up and were now non-existent. Bills began to be paid later and later. Debt balances crept up higher and higher. All the while, as they watched their finances take a tumble right before their very eyes, stress levels were skyrocketing, and worry was setting in. When a household's main breadwinner, my father, goes from making over $100k a year to barely making $30k a year, it changes EVERYTHING. However, things didn't stop there; this event flowed into yet another event on my financial education journey.

At the ripe young age of 21, I found out that someone had stolen my identity. To make matters worse, I soon found out that the identity-stealing culprit was a family member, of all people. At the time,

I was taking a management class at Georgia Southern University. As an extra credit assignment, our professor asked us to check our credit reports using the annualcreditreport.com website, which provides consumers with a free credit report from each of the three top bureaus in America. Thanks to the Fair Credit Reporting Act, in an attempt to protect and provide transparency for the consumer, every individual is entitled to one free copy of his or her report per year.

I will be forever grateful that my professor prompted us to check our credit reports. When I checked mine, I was surprised to discover that I had one credit card open in my name that I knew nothing about and another credit card in my name that had somehow accumulated a balance of about $4,000 in charges that I did not authorize! I was totally devastated about this, in addition to being angry and feeling an ultimate sense of betrayal. After all, family members are supposed to be the people that you can trust the most, above all others in the world. As a result, when they betray your trust and confidence in their abilities to look out for and protect you, the wound goes deep. I'm not completely naïve; I know that no family – and no individual – is perfect. However, I simply could not believe that such a thing could happen to me; but just like the rest of the 10 million Americans it happens to every year, it did indeed happen to me. It was at this point that I learned another rich lesson on my financial education journey: I needed to better monitor my credit.

Even amongst all that had happened to me thus far on my journey, the true importance of maintaining my own personal finances did not register in my mind. I was in my own little "college student bubble", making enough money to pay my bills, working part-time in the Resource Management Department as a co-op with the U.S. Army Corps of Engineers, and enjoying the luxury of having my parents assist me with paying half of my rent.

It was not until after I graduated from college that I set off to become fully engaged as an adult on my financial education journey.

I graduated from Georgia Southern University in Statesboro, Georgia in December of 2009 with dual degrees in accounting and finance. Upon graduating, I moved to Savannah, Georgia, where my job with the U.S. Army Corps of Engineers was located. Per the co-op program, I was to start out making approximately $38k a year, with a salary bump up to $48k after one year, and a final bump up to $56k after two years. To keep my rent costs down, I shared an apartment with a roommate, who was also a recent college grad starting with the Corps of Engineers.

Prior to moving to Savannah, I signed up to take a CPA preparation course. I figured that since I had just finished college, now would be the best time to continue to study for my CPA license – while my study habits were still fresh. That prep course cost me about $4,000, which I didn't have, so I financed it through the company that was offering the course. Then, the exam itself was another $1,000. Again, I did not have the money, so I borrowed the amount from my local credit union.

After a month of working at my job with the Corps of Engineers, my typical American consumer behavior began to show. Since it was late January, Super Bowl XLIII was right around the corner. At the time, I had a 26-inch LCD Samsung television; however, this TV, which was perfectly fine in college, all of a sudden become too small and highly unsuitable for watching the Pittsburgh Steelers battle the Arizona Cardinals in the biggest game of the year. I simply could not watch the Super Bowl on such a small television, especially because it was not L.E.D., which was the latest technology at the time. Thus, armed with the ever-familiar, "I just graduated from college, so I deserve this" rationale, I headed on down to my local Best Buy store, where I found a $2,800 television – that was, coincidentally put on sale just in time for the Super Bowl – for $1,800! As discounted as the high-tech beauty was, I didn't have the money at the time; thus, I opened up a Best Buy credit card, which offered me an attractive 0% interest over the next 18 months. With 0% interest, I figured that this was free money, and I was confident that I would eventually pay it back before the 18 month period ended. The sad thing is that I didn't even watch the game on my brand new, expensive television set that night - I ended up going to a local sports bar instead.

After working at my new job with the Corps of Engineers as a part-time intern for eight months and then being hired as a full-time employee (which I admit paid me a respectable salary), after a few months, I realized that I was already living from paycheck to paycheck. This realization became clear because I was always looking forward to the next payday: the day that I would have more money to spend to take care of my responsibilities and to spend at my own discretion. As I would spend time mentally calculating how much I would get, where the money would be spent, and how much I would have left to spend on things I wanted to do, places I wanted to go, and people I wanted to please, it struck me that I was following in my parents' footsteps. I was spending my money before I ever received it, and I knew, without any uncertainty, that this was a bad practice.

Before this season of my life, I used to think that my parents lived from paycheck to paycheck because they were not born in the United States; they were immigrants that had come to the U.S. from Ghana. In my mind, it was their lack of familiarity with the way that money, the finance system, creditors, etc. worked that made them vulnerable to making such mistakes. "Otherwise, why would they ever allow themselves to be put into such a vulnerable situation as to be living from paycheck to paycheck?" I reasoned. However, I now had my answer, and I was humbled by it, because here I was now following in the same footsteps.

Sadly, even though I was already living from paycheck to pay-check, I was still determined to purchase the brand new 2011 Mustang GT 5.0, which had just started rolling off of the assembly line, for myself. In fact, despite my shaky financial position, I was so determined to get behind the wheel of one of these powerful driving machines that I went to the Ford website and custom built my own Mustang! I printed out a picture of my shiny new design and pasted it on my cubicle wall as my daily motivation; my determination to have it grew with each glance I cast towards it.

It was at this time that a couple of my co-workers, now my beloved friends, Jesse King and Jason Jarret, intervened. During this time, they had been trying to convince me that I needed to stay away from debt and only pay for things that I could afford with cash; they swore to me that making such a decision would change my life forever. Despite their persistence to help guide my financial future in the right direction, I politely blew them off every time they would start such a conversation. I wanted the things that I wanted, when I wanted them – whether I could afford them with cash or not – and the way of life that these guys were proposing, would mean deferring my gratification until I actually had the money in hand to spend on things. As many things as I wanted, and as much time as it would take to be able to afford them with cash, I simply could not see living life their way. Though I ultimately did not get the Mustang, I still continued to live life my way – a decision that would turn out to be a costly mistake.

Shortly after life started happening, my car needed tires; however, I did not have the money to purchase them, since I was living from paycheck to paycheck. Thus, I did what every normal American would do -, I opened up a Firestone credit card for my $600 tire purchase and installation. With each new credit application; each new credit card received; each new charge that I accrued; and each statement in the mail reminding me of all of the money that I owed my debtors, I began to feel more and more – and more – broke. I was beyond living from paycheck to paycheck, because what I was bringing home in my paycheck was not even making ends meet. My eyes were just now opening to the seriousness of my financial situation, and I did not like what I was seeing.

I remember one month in particular when I did not have enough money to pay my full portion of the rent without compromising my ability to pay my other bills. I kindly asked my roommate if he would pay my portion of the rent, and I would pay him back with my next paycheck – and he kindly declined. In retrospect, I don't blame him. I was on a sinking ship of debt, and there was no reason for him to have confidence that I would repay him when I said I would. Little did I know, but my roommate's refusal to rescue me from the mess that I had made with my financial mismanagement would be one of the best things to ever happen to me.

This moment marked a pivotal moment for me on my financial journey, for it was at this time that I finally started feeling tired of being broke. I was finally fed up with it! It was also at this time that I knew that I needed to do something about my financial situation; there was no way that I would ever be able to prosper financially if my money was constantly going out of the door without my being able to save any of it. I was finally starting to think ahead and see the proverbial light that was being shed on my financial mentality. How could I ever be the future leader of a household, retire with dignity, and powerfully impact the community around me, if I continued living like this?

Being trapped in this endless debt cycle was beginning to add a level of stress to my life that I could not bear. I had to find a way to do something different with my money, because I was now repeating the mistakes of my parents; I didn't want to get into things so deeply that I experienced their same outcomes, so I needed to make some changes now! The first step to my financial rehabilitation consisted of several steps that led to my standing before my friends Jesse and Jason with a humble admission that I had made a mess of my financial life and an appeal for help. They introduced me to Dave Ramsey, an advocate of basic personal finance that is based less on theory and more on practical, common sense. This turned out to be just the direction I needed.

Armed with the new knowledge that I was learning from Dave Ramsey, I now had a foundation upon which to build a new financial life. Before long, my financial empowerment process was underway. I developed and lived according to a budget, I built a starter emergency fund, and then I started eliminating my debt. At the time, I had accumulated more than $26,000 in debt. Things were looking up for me, and I was excited about the possibilities of living a life free of the financial bondage that I had created for myself.

One of the methods that I was living by in order to become debt-free was that of the "debt snowball". With this method, I concentrated on paying off my smallest debts first, while making minimum payments on my other accounts. Once the smallest debt is completely paid off, the monies that were being used for that debt would then be used to attack the next smallest debt, and so on. With this method, the goal was to knock out the debt that I had with each one of my creditors, from smallest to largest. As I was six months into my debt snowball, I was blessed with the first $10,000 step-up in annual salary; this represented an extra $385 per paycheck. Prior to my new financial education, I would have easily found a way to spend that extra money. However now, I used it as part of my artillery to attack my debt. This extra firepower came in handy and at just the right time!

Around the same time, an opportunity to work overtime by help-ing another Army Corps division within the agency came about. Thomas Edison said, "Opportunity is missed by most people be-cause it is dressed in overalls and looks like work." I find this to be very true. I capitalized on this opportunity, working upwards of 68 hours per week over a four-month period. I remember thinking, "It's amazing how God works when you make intentional efforts to better handle the money placed in your possession!" Without this overtime opportunity, it would have taken me at least two and a half to three years to get out of debt. Yes, working all of those extra hours was not fun at all, but the sacrifices and hard work paid off; I was able to dou-ble my income from $2,000 a month to $4,000 a month during that period. With a focused mind and a strong game plan, I had success-fully eliminated all of my debt by June 9, 2011 – within 11 months of starting my debt-elimination process! At the time of the writing of this book, I have been debt free for three and half years, and life has been amazing! I have a fully-funded emergency fund and a strong retirement fund. Best of all, I have seen my net worth increase 680%!

Along my journey to financial empowerment, I have learned some valuable lessons and have experienced life in a whole new way. For example, I have experienced how being financially empowered has not only changed my financial condition, but it has positively impact-ed my mental attitude and my priorities in life. I have learned that life is not just about making money, but rather about asking myself what I can do with the money I earn and how I can use it to impact the lives of others. If life had been just about money, I would have stayed in the accounting industry, making up to $90,000 a year with my cur-rent level of experience. Instead, I am now following my passion and fulfilling my purpose by sharing the valuable financial knowledge that I have attained through my own financial coaching company.

I am on a purposeful and meaningful mission to help people become financially empowered to take control of their lives, because I firmly believe that when you get your finances in order, you will get your life in order. Because I believe so passionately in it, I will not stop my pursuit of this mission until I am six feet under! As you navigate your way through this book, it is my hope that you will become empowered financially by eliminating financial stress, by being able to truly sleep well at night, by being able to do the "little" things like finally taking your car to the auto repair so they can tell you the reason that your check engine light has been on for a year – and fix the problem – so that you can stop worrying about being on the side of the road, and even "little" things like finally being able to go to the doctor and admit to the unusual symptoms that you have been experiencing for several months, because now you can afford to pay for the tests! Changing your financial condition will indeed change your life. It is my goal to help you experience these changes in your life so that your ability to live out your dreams, pursue your ambitions, and address the "little" things that make a big impact on life will one day be a reality!

CHAPTER 2
It's Called "Personal Finance" for a Reason!

Analyzing and addressing one's personal finances – along with the budgeting, saving, planning, and forecasting that it involves – carries a connotation of being very complicated. In fact, over my years of experience as a financial coach, I have learned that people consider personal finance so complicated that they do not even want to talk about or face the reality of their financial situation. Having to stand face-to-face to confront their levels of brokenness and debt that they themselves have created as a result of their personal appetites, is just too devastating of an experience for them. Further, when coupled with having to develop a strategy of how to climb their way out of their bleak situation, the experience seems to be too complex and overwhelming for them to bear. It's simply too much reality for them! Thus, rather than seek help, most people choose to take the ostrich approach, burying their heads in the sand and hoping the problem will somehow go away on its own. My friend, that's simply not going to happen!

Allow me to open your eyes to the truth of the matter. Personal finance only seems to be complicated because it is so personal to us. It is one of the most intimate aspects of who we really are! However, in reality, it is not complicated at all. If you will allow the principles of financial empowerment to impact your financial behaviors rather than many of your personal characteristics that currently impact them, you will find that you will walk into a financial future that is not complicated at all. In fact, you will find your finances quite simple and easy to address!

Financial Freedom is Not about How Well You Can

Calculate –

It's about How Well You Can Personally Behave!

Oftentimes, those people who are bold enough to confront the gloomy state of their finances will find themselves instantly coming to a resolve of, "No problem! I'll just calculate better and make sure that I am more intentional about how much money I make versus how much money I spend. Problem solved!" However, only a few steps into their journey, the will find themselves among the millions of other people who have also tried to repair their finances by treating it as a numbers game – and failed miserably.

The truth is that how well you do with money is not just a numbers game; it is not all about math. If personal finances were simply about math, people would not be in the desperate financial situation that most are in today; they would not be spending more than they make or living from paycheck to paycheck. Any person six years-old or older can tell you that $3,500 minus $3,500 equals zero. Yet, for some reason, we have a nation of people that spend more than they bring home on a regular basis in order to maintain lifestyles that they cannot afford. No, personal financial management is not about numbers; it is about behavior. In fact your ability to manage your personal finances successfully is 80% behavior and 20% head knowledge.

The primary reason that the world of personal finance is so "personal" is because what shapes the personal finance context of one person, differs from what shapes the personal finance context of another. Each person's context, experiences, and influences are unique to the individual himself. Among the key influences that impact the world of personal finance in which each of us live are: your relationships; your environment; and your social/cultural groups; as well as other physical, emotional, environmental, intellectual, and spiritual factors.

Relationships

Your relationships impact your finances because they dictate, in large part, with or upon whom you spend your money. We can all relate to this! How we spend money when we are single, without a girlfriend or boyfriend is different from how we spend money when we have one. How we spend money when we are married is different from how we spend money when we are not married. Whether it's spending money on a vacation for you and your partner versus you alone; or whether it's spending money for a pizza as you enjoy a simple movie night alone at your place versus going to a nice restaurant with a boyfriend or girlfriend. Those with whom you have relationships with impacts your personal finances.

Environment

Your environment impacts your finances because it affects your decisions concerning what you might think is worthy of spending money on and what is not. Different environments demand different types of expenses from those who live within it. For example, someone who lives in Chicago might have to spend money on snow tires while buying snow tires would never even cross the mind of someone living in Miami. However, someone living in Miami might instead have to spend money on flood or hurricane insurance while the person in Chicago would not.

Social/Cultural Context

We've all heard the saying, "Birds of a feather flock together". Right? Well this concept is especially true as it pertains to the issue of personal finance. Your social or cultural practices can have a strong influence in dictating what you spend your money on and how you spend it. For example, in some cultures, when your parents become elderly and cannot live independently and on their own, it is believed that their children are obligated to move their parents into their own homes and take care of them. According to the cultural norm, this is grounded in the belief that this is a reasonable act of gratitude for what the parents have done for their children, in giving them life; raising them; and supporting them throughout their lives. However, in other cultures, this expectation is not strongly present. According to societal norms, when parents age, it is perfectly acceptable for their children to place them in a retirement home and visit them from time to time.

If you live in a culture in which children bring their aged parents in to live with them, this would likely cause the household to have higher grocery expenses; utility costs; and possibly even higher medical expenses. However, if your aged parents were placed in a retirement home, this too could possibly affect your finances. For instance, there are potentially costs associated with living in the retirement home that the parents might not be able to cover; these would fall on you. There are also other costs to consider like gas for trips to visit your parents, gifts and supplies that you will bring during your visits to the retirement home and other incidental expenses. Both of these scenarios depend on your parents' financial position and their insurance coverage at the time that such decisions need to be made.

Another way in which social practices or conditioning might affect your finances surrounds the type of car that you drive. Did you know that who your friends are or what area of town you live in can strongly influence the kind of car you drive. It is a sad truth to admit, but I personally know plenty of people who have purchased luxury cars like BMW's and Mercedes Benz's, even though they could not necessarily afford the car payments, insurance, and repairs of maintaining such high-class vehicles. However, in their drives to be perceived as successful by their friends and neighbors, they made these purchases. After all, if you drive one of these luxury cars, it automatically means that you are financially successful, right? Spending a ton of money on your car (especially ones that are costly to maintain) is the single most prevalent wealth snatcher of the middle class. Cars depreciate, or go down in value, like a rock! In order to build wealth, you should not invest a lot in things that go down in value; you should invest in things that go up in value! One of the greatest pieces of advice that I can give you is to be comfortable with who you are and the level of success that you have attained today. Continue building and striving to live according to sound financial principles, and one day, you will be able to actually afford and maintain the luxury items that you want – that is, if you still value them by then!

People who buy things that they cannot afford, for the sake of being perceived as successful, are simply trying to keep up with the Joneses. However, I know the Joneses. In fact, several of the Joneses have been clients of mine, so I know their financial condition intimately. I'm going to let you in on a little secret that no one else – including the Joneses – has told you: the Joneses are broke! Yes, they have a nice house, but the high mortgage is stressing them out, so it's hard to enjoy their luxury living quarters. Yes, they have nice, luxury cars with monthly car note payments the size of many other people's mortgages, but they are praying that they do not break down, because they do not have the means to fix the cars if they do. Yes, they post pictures on social media of their elaborate vacations to faraway places, but they are still paying for the trip years later, because they charged it on a credit card. Don't be fooled by the Joneses; their households are filled with tremendous stress and anxiety, and maintaining such a façade of true wealth and success is downright exhausting!

Physical Condition

Though most people never stop to consider the impact that their physical condition has on their money, the truth is that our physical condition really does have a strong influence on our finances. Of course, there is the obvious example of this relationship: if one has a disability of some sort, he or she will spend more on medical bills, treatments, medication, rehabilitative therapy, etc. However, let's focus on the less obvious examples that tend to pertain to the larger population.

The less obvious example of the influence that our physical condition has on our spending, is best illustrated by examining the life of someone who is healthy and fit versus someone who is unhealthy and of poor health. A person who is healthy and fit might spend more money on organic foods; whole, unprocessed foods (which tend to cost more); vitamin supplements; and a gym membership. A person who is unfit and of poor health might spend more money on fast food, doctor visits, and prescription medications, and he or she might miss more days of work, which often results in less take-home pay.

Our physical condition not only impacts our expenses, but it also impacts our revenue – our ability to generate income at work. For example, when you feel better physically, you are able to contribute more time, energy, and focus towards the things in life that really matter, including your marital and family relationships, friendships, hobbies, spirituality, etc. As a result, you are happier and more productive, and this makes you a better worker! In turn, better workers get promoted faster and make more money, which results in your ability to generate more income or revenue. Needless to say, if some people were in better physical condition, their finances would also improve. Thus, our physical condition has a significant and direct impact on our finances in more ways than we tend to realize.

Emotions

Emotions play a big role in how we manage our finances because we are emotional beings; at any given time of day, each and every one of us is feeling some sort of emotion. We also decide, act, and spend money every day based upon how we feel emotionally. For example, when we make purchases, whether we realize it or not, our decisions are almost always emotional. For example, have you ever heard of an "impulse buy" – something you had not planned to buy, but you saw it, desired it, and immediately had to have it, so you bought it? Emotions are the drivers that are at the very center of each and every impulse buy you make!

It is commonplace in our society to hear women (and occasionally even men!) say that they need to get out to do some "retail therapy". When they are happy, they shop. When they are sad, they shop. Even when they are perfectly fine, they shop! What is clearly at the center of this? Emotions! Spending money on things that we want and need – even though we might not be able to actually afford them – has a way of changing our emotional state and making us feel better. In this case, not only do our emotions impact our spending, but a cycle is created in which spending, in turn, affects our emotions.

No one understands better than retailers how emotions affect our spending habits. Retailers understand that we are emotional beings. In fact, they pour billions of dollars into research, in their efforts to determine how to appeal to people – and their emotions – to prompt them to spend more. Everything in a store, from the music that is playing, to the layout of the store, has been strategically staged, designed and manipulated in such a way that it sends a clear message to the consumer: "Buy this!" For instance, when is the last time you went into a grocery store to buy diapers? Have you ever noticed that they tend to always position the aisle for the baby diapers near the alcohol? There is a reason for this! Research suggests that when shoppers go into a grocery store to buy diapers, for reasons that might be obvious to some and not so obvious to others, they also bought beer and wine! With this, the grocery retailers are simply saying, "We know how you feel!" Nothing in a retail shopping experience is ever by coincidence; everything about it is strategically designed to appeal to your emotions.

The next time you go into a store, take a moment or two to notice that the music is often upbeat. They will often be playing selections that strike an emotional chord or that will make you bob your head saying, "I love this song!" They play songs that make you happy. Why? Because research indicates that people spend more money when they are happy or upbeat!

Take a store like Old Navy, for example, which is a clothing retailer designed to appeal to the younger trendy generation. It would be a bad idea for Old Navy to play classical music in its stores. Not only does it not fit the fun, trendy environment, but it is not the kind of music that would make its target consumer demographic happy. In other words, young people would not walk into their stores and say, "This classical tune is my favorite!" Instead, such music would have an opposite effect and cause sales to plummet!

Intellectual

Intellect is considered to be a person's ability to learn and reason, or one's capacity for knowledge and understanding. The more financial intelligence you possess, the more capacity you will have to be able to positively manage your personal finances. The less financial intelligence you possess, the less of a capacity you will have to be able to manage your personal finances.

For example, for many who seek to learn information that will increase their financial intelligence, once they learn that they can live a life that is free of debt, their thought patterns about how they relate to money change forever. However, if a person never seeks new information about how to manage his finances, his level of financial intelligence will stay the same – and so will his financial condition.

There is a considerable difference between what an informed consumer will experience when making a major purchase versus that of an uninformed consumer. The informed consumer has equipped himself with the intelligence that he needs to successfully negotiate the lowest price for the greatest value. However, the uninformed consumer, armed only with the same knowledge he has always used when making a major purchase, is prone to getting the same value that he has always gotten: one that benefits the retailer and not him as a consumer. Our knowledge and understanding – the intelligence – surrounding the process, or the lack thereof, will significantly impact what we walk away with, as consumers.

For example, consider how intelligence plays a role when we make one of the most major decisions that we tend to make: the purchase of a car. Informed consumers know that it is better to buy a used car that is two to three years old, because they do not depreciate, or lose their value, as quickly as new cars do. Informed consumers also know that they will get a better deal if they buy from a private owner than from a car dealership. Dealerships must mark-up the price of their vehicles in order to cover the overhead of their business. Informed consumers will know that it is smart to have a trusted mechanic check out the used car before they make the purchase. Lastly, informed consumers will know to approach the purchase of a car with a budget of how much they are going to spend and not allow a sweet-talking dealer or private car seller to get the best of them, convincing them to spend more than they planned, which would inevitably result in buyer's remorse. Intelligence can play a major role in helping consumers spend their money better!

A problem can never be fixed using the same mindset that created it. Thus, it is only when we know better that we can do better. However, we will never be equipped to do a better job with our finances if we do not seek new information, or intelligence, that is needed to do so. Simply put, knowing more about how money works, helps us to spend our money better!

Spiritual

Our spiritual beliefs help define our morals, values, and principles in life. Because they shape our mentality, they will inevitably affect the way that we relate to our money. Each of us has a spirit, so we are all spiritual beings, whether we consider ourselves to be "spiritual" or not. However, we are all at different places in our spiritual development and on our spiritual journey, and where we are has a direct impact on how we relate to money.

For example, one individual who is passionate about his spirituality and believes that it is his spiritual responsibility to give of his finances, might deem it important to donate a certain percentage of his income to his place of worship, while another person who is not as spiritually engaged and who does not regularly attend a place of worship, does not. One person might consider it to be important to give more of his money to help support a spiritual institution, while another might consider it to be more important to accumulate more of his money for himself and his family. Regardless of what spiritual beliefs we possess – and we all possess them, whether they are defined or not – and live according to, we must be careful to understand that they do affect our financial decisions. Thus, an awareness of what you stand for, spiritually, is important.

Each of the seven influences that make personal finance "personal" is intertwined; no one influence is a standalone, but both impacts and is impacted by, each of the other influences. Thus, regardless of what you believe, the truth is that money is indeed personal, because it is influenced by so many different dimensions of your life!

Feelings and Financial Progress DO NOT Go

Together:

Learning to Live According to Principles!

Moving forward, if you want to be financially successful, you must learn to stop making money decisions and behaviors based upon how you feel! I know that you don't feel like creating or following a budget. I know that you don't feel like addressing your student loan debt. I know that you don't feel like picking up a second job to generate income. However, these are simply your feelings talking; if you were to tap into your rational mind, it would say, Yes! We need a budget! We need to confront our student loan debt! Go get that second job! One resolve that you will need to make on your journey to financial success, is that of allowing your rational mind, which operates out of sound financial principles, to speak to you more loudly than your feelings!

The truth is that we have no business putting real stock into our feelings, because they can tend to be flighty; in a split second, they can change with the wind. Our feelings are in a constant state of flux, changing in one direction or another based upon our current situation in life. Since life is constantly changing, our feelings are constantly changing with it. Thus, when we consider how unpredictable life is, and consequently, how unpredictable our feelings can be, should we really be basing some of the most critical decisions of our financial lives on our feelings? The answer is no.

Every decision that we make regarding our finances should be based upon principle. Why? Because at the end of your feelings is nothing worth having, but at the end of your principles is a promise. Principles, which are our firm beliefs, attitudes, laws, rules, stand as fundamental truths in our lives that are not up for compromise. Unlike emotions, they do not fluctuate, waiver, or change depending upon life's circumstances. Instead, they remain firm and true regardless of what conditions or situations we encounter in life.

For example a principle that I live by is, "The borrower is slave to the lender". This saying comes from the Bible in Proverbs 22:7. I firmly believe in this principle, and because of my belief in it. I will always work to ensure that I am not in the position of being a borrower. I do not ever want to be someone else's slave again. Since attaining my financial freedom, I can now look back over my young years and see the impact – the blinding chokehold – that debt had on me. I remember how, when I was in debt, I was so driven about how much money I made; regardless of what I made, I was never satisfied. Now, I am at peace; I do not need to make a lot of money in order to be happy. Since becoming financially free, I have found that as long as I am enjoying what I am doing and have the ability to spend time on things I want to be doing, I am completely satisfied. My financial freedom has also allowed me the freedom to think more about my life and what I want out of it. I honestly feel like I am on an entirely different level than I was when I was in debt.

I could not have attained and sustained my current level of financial freedom without living according to principle. My firm resolve to live according to the principle of not being a borrower, is one that has helped me to realize the life that I have always desired to live. It is for this very reason that you should strive to live your life, not according to your emotions, but according to principle; at the end of principles is reward, while at the end of your feelings is failure.

By which principles do you live? What are the firm beliefs guiding your life and your financial management that you will refuse to compromise, regardless of what circumstances you might face? You should take some time to seriously identify or establish firm, unshakable principles to which you will hold yourself as you begin this financial empowerment process. As someone who has been through the process and coached countless others through it over the years, I can tell you without reservation that you're going to need them! This process of financial recovery will test you at your very limits, so you will need a good set of principles to keep you on the path to success, both financially and in life!

Along this journey, I will encourage you to allow your principles – not your emotions – to drive the new financial behaviors that you will learn. You will find that the financial empowerment process that I offer is geared towards helping you to reshape your behaviors into the behaviors of those who win with money and win with their lives. However, your behaviors will mean nothing if they are not coupled with principles; the two must operate hand in hand. With a commitment to allowing your principles to drive your new financial behaviors, I guarantee that you will get in control of your money, and consequently, get in control of your life!

CHAPTER 3
Who Are You When It Comes to Managing Money?

Who are you really? I'm not asking how your family, friends, and co-workers define you. I'm asking who you are – the real you – the essence of who you are that is comprised of how you are, and what you like, think, believe, and value? What makes you tick? What makes you you? When I pose this seemingly fundamental question to my clients, there is often a long pause; they really have to think about it! One of the primary reasons for our lack of true identity, is that society does not place a strong emphasis on helping people to discover who they really are. However, it is my firm belief that before people can really become successful, they must understand themselves.

Discovering who you are allows you to understand enough about yourself to be able to engage life in a way that works specifically for you most effectively. Think of all of the successful people that you know who are prospering in life. Successful people always seem to have the ability to make decisions that propel them to greater and greater levels in life? Have you ever wondered why? One key reason that they are able to manage their lives so effectively is because they know their true selves; they know what works best for them; and they know what it takes for them to be effective. They take all of this knowledge into consideration when making life decisions, and as a result, they produce outcomes that are custom-tailored for the successful lives they desire to lead!

To become knowledgeable about ourselves, we must engage in consistent, intentional efforts that are designed for self-development, including reading books; attending seminars; and engaging in times of self-reflection. However, this approach towards self-development and self-awareness is not limited to our lives in general. The same approach should be used in a narrower way to help us to become more aware of who we are when dealing with our finances and help us to become more financially developed and empowered. Such knowledge of who we are financially is vital to our ability to attain financial success, because it will help us to make decisions that are most effective for us as individuals!

The Two Types of Financial Personalities

Each and every one of us has a financial personality. Unfortunately, most of us do not know our financial personality, because such an identity is neither taught in our public education system, nor is it discussed within our society. More than likely, the reason that most remain quiet on the topic is because the issue of how to best manage one's personal finances is a hot-button issue – one of great debate. Some would even put it on the level of religion and politics - other issues that people choose not to talk about because of the volatile nature of the topic. Think about it: if someone invited you over to dinner, you wouldn't sit at the table and bring up personal, controversial topics like religion and politics, would you? In the same way, you would not dare bring up the topic of personal finances, because this is such a very sensitive topic that could easily ruin everyone's evening – especially when people's finances are in such terrible shape!

The truth is that if we started teaching about personal finance and financial personality early-on, integrating it into our education system, people would have a greater awareness of what their money management tendencies were and be able to watch out for the financial pitfalls that are waiting for them. Equipping people with such knowledge about themselves would significantly reduce many of the financial mistakes that most Americans make in their younger years – all because they understood themselves. Even better, just by being armed with the tool of understanding their financial personalities, many people would be positioned to incur less debt, have a higher net worth, and have more stable financial futures.

Despite the hush-hush nature with which our society tends to approach the issue of personal finance, I equate the importance of knowing your financial personality type to that of knowing your family history. Knowledge of your financial personality type gives you a good understanding of how your upbringing has impacted your current money habits; what tendencies and habits you tend to lean towards when making money decisions; and how you think overall, concerning money as a result of your nature, nurture, and exposure. This knowledge is beneficial, because it helps to guide you towards making better financial decisions; ones that take into consideration each of these factors and chooses a path that is most effective for you to attain your financial goals. After all, you cannot know where you are going if you do not know where you currently stand. Becoming aware of your financial personality helps you to know exactly where you are today, so that you can choose the best path for moving forward in the right direction.

The Saver vs. the Spender

There are two types of financial personalities: the saver and the spender. Spenders behave exactly as their name implies; they are very good at spending money, but have a very difficult time saving. Spenders, spend so well, in fact, that they have usually already spent their entire paycheck before it comes in the door! They also tend to be generous, as they have no problem spending their money on others. Having often spent all of their money to the point that they are down to almost nothing, Spenders are typically those who eagerly look forward to payday so that they can start living again!

The Saver is the exact opposite of the Spender. These individuals have a natural ability to save. For Savers, accumulating cash through saving is as easy as pie; they do it like clockwork. In fact, the frugal behavior of Savers is the reason why banks have money to lend to others (who are more than likely Spenders)! Savers rarely spend their hard-earned income outside of what is required for basic necessities, and when a situation arises in which they have to spend a good amount of money, like a major car repair, they have trouble sleeping at night. They do not like to let go of their money!

To Spenders, Savers might seem like they don't have a life. To Savers, Spenders might appear to be careless and irresponsible. However, a peculiar relationship tends to exist among these two financial personality types: for better or worse they tend to marry each other! We have all heard the saying that "opposites attract"; when it comes to financial personalities this statement is applicable in most cases!

As surprising a relationship as it might seem, the truth is that Savers and Spenders both need one another. Spenders need Savers so that they can achieve long-term financial goals, such as retiring and not having to eat Ramen noodles every day for the rest of their lives! Savers need Spenders so that they can have a life! Indeed, if it wasn't for Spenders, the only time Savers would go out and spend money would be at annual savings conventions!

In the rare case that a relationship is made up of two Spenders, the couple will most likely never have any money; they spend everything they get, and neither one is disciplined enough to save. The opposite is also true. If a couple is made up of two Savers, they will most likely always have money in savings; however, they will have a much harder time enjoying life and spending their money on having fun.

The Nerd vs. The Free Spirit

The distinctions in financial personality do not stop with Saver vs. Spender. Both the Spender and Saver can be broken down into two sub-categories: the Nerd and the Free Spirit. A Spender might be a Nerd, or he might be a Free Spirit. Sometimes, a Spender is a little of both but can usually identify with one category more than the other. The same applies to a Saver. A Saver might be a Nerd, he might be a Free Spirit, or he might be a little of both. More likely than not, if you're a Saver then you're probably also the Nerd, but that's not always the case.

Nerds enjoy putting together the monthly budget and calculating the numbers. They like that it gives them control, and they feel like they are taking care of their loved ones by responsibly fulfilling these functions. Nerds also need to have a financial plan laid out; like to watch the accounts; tend to be numbers oriented; and have no problem staring at spreadsheets and analyzing numbers all day long.

On the other hand, Free Spirits just want to have fun. They don't want anything to do with the numbers. They have no desire to keep up with checking or other accounts, tend to "forget" about the budget, and, in many cases, they like to bless others as much as they can.

To a Nerd, a Free Spirit might seem to be irresponsible. To a Free Spirit, a Nerd might appear to be controlling and uncaring.

Knowing Your Financial Personality Can Lead to

a Happier, Healthier Relationship!

If you are single, it is important for you to understand your financial personality. However, if you are in a marital relationship, the necessity of you and your partner both being aware of and understanding your respective financial personalities is important at an even greater level. Knowing your natural spending and saving tendencies will help you to understand each other better and will inherently help you to manage your money as a couple better as well.

Oftentimes, when couples can learn and understand one another's financial personalities, they tend to work better together financially. What's more, since money touches every area of our lives, understanding each spouse's tendencies when it comes to money, results in improved communication. With increased understanding, both spouses tend to work together in order to achieve their financial goals. This ultimately results in a happier marriage! In fact, most of the couples that I personally coach through the financial empowerment process, report that their marriage drastically improved after they understood their partners' personalities. They finally began to work together on their finances as opposed to working against each other.

Note: If you are still unsure of what your financial personality might be, in the back of this book we have included a 6-question assessment that will help you identify which personality you are.

CHAPTER 4

What's Your "Why"?

Why, exactly, is it that you do what you do? Why is it that you get out of bed every morning? Why is it that you even bought this book? These are all important questions to ask yourself, and more importantly, they are important questions for you to answer about yourself. In fact, take a few seconds to think about your answers!

Your ability to engage in such a level of self-reflection and self-analysis is critical if you will attain any level of success, including financial success, in life. Why? Because it helps you to get down to the fundamental motivation behind what you are doing – your main purpose for engaging in each decision you make and each action you undertake. Asking yourself questions like these, questions that cause you to really assess and discover your "Why?" empower you with the most powerful tool and resource available to keep you going. What's your "Why?"

Human beings are the most powerful creatures ever to roam the face of the earth. I say this because people are consistently finding new and creative ways to use resources; constantly developing new technologies; and taking an active role in developing and inventing things that most would deem impossible – until they are accomplished. Due to many of the innovations in our society, we have now discovered more efficient and convenient ways to carry out many of the functions that are a part of our everyday lives. Then, there are some tasks that we do not even carry out anymore, like sending telegrams or buying film for cameras, because as a result of technology, they have become obsolete.

None of the vast technological achievements and innovative inventions that we enjoy today could have gone from idea to reality without someone having a vision; in the mind's eye of just one person, it was just as possible as any other reality that surrounded him or her, regardless of how unthinkable others might have thought the idea to be. Visions help to propel us towards the achievement of great things; before you can achieve anything great – including financial freedom – you must have a vision. You must be able to see it happening, and it must be so real to you that despite others' inability to see it, you pursue it with all you've got, because you know it can happen! Simply put, a vision is your "Why?" and with a Why, anything is possible! As you embark upon this financial empowerment journey, it is going to be critical that you know and understand your Why. Your Why will be that which drives you to keep moving and that which allows you to keep punching when times get tough – and they will.

The Sacrifices You Will Soon Make Require

Knowing Your "Why"!

One of my favorite quotes of all time is one that I heard while watching the movie in the Transformers franchise. In the movie, Sam Witwicky, a character played by actor Shia LaBeouf, said, "No sacrifice, no victory". That simple quote comprised of four little words resonated deeply with me from the moment I heard them; in fact, it has been seven years since I heard the quote, and it has been permanently embedded into my psyche and affects every aspect of my lifestyle. Why? Because it made complete sense! In fact, seventy percent of the Forbes 400 started out with nothing, and each individual on the list became one of the wealthiest people in America. This just goes to show that you don't have to be born into money to end up with wealth; you just have to be willing to do what it takes to get there. Without sacrifice, there will be no victory! Without sacrifice, there can never be success!

When I consider all of the successful leaders, athletes, and entrepreneurs of the past and present, I realize that all of them had something in common: they ALL made sacrifices to get where they wanted to be. Success comes from sacrificing your time, your energy, and your resources, as well as a strong resolve to bounce back from failure, push yourself to new heights, endure things you don't like, in order to get to where you want to be, and continue to move forward, when even those who are closest to you do not even believe in you. To make those sacrifices you need to have a Why.

The Life of Freedom You're Striving Towards

Requires Knowing Your "Why"!

Financial freedom is a state of being in a financial position in which you have personal liberties available to you: you can afford to make your way out of unhealthy work environments and away from bad bosses and other unpleasant situations. You can travel, start a business, and/or volunteer as much and anywhere you would like. It's tough to do the things that you really want to do when you're worried about making your next mortgage, student loan, car note, or credit card payment!

Currently, the middle and lower income classes are controlled by employment, government, and other higher-level entities that regulate what they can and cannot do with their lives. However, you are not relegated to being included in that number. You have the power to change your life by changing the way you relate to your finances! You no longer have to be controlled by anything except what you desire to do. You can become financially free and wake up every day to options instead of mandates. Ultimately, acquiring great wealth is not about showing off all of your excess money; it is about creating choices and options that are pleasing and fulfilling to you. However, be warned, this life of financial freedom that you will soon begin striving to live, requires a very good understanding of your Why!

I wish I could tell you that the financial empowerment process is easy. I wish I could tell you that you will be able to get by with minimal effort and that you will become easily wealthy. I wish I could tell you that you won't have to change your lifestyle much. In fact, I actually could tell you all of these things, but I would be lying – and lying is not an option when I'm coaching my clients. The truth of the matter is that because we are going to be addressing your financial behaviors, it will be a challenging process.

As human beings, we are creatures of habit, so I am pretty sure that you have been managing your money a certain way for quite some time now. Anytime you attempt to break a habit or routine, it is a difficult task. That is why it is so hard for you, if you never work out, to start working out. After you begin working out and exercising regularly, it is even more difficult to keep going. However, once you get to a point where working out is a part of your routine, you actually feel guilty if you miss a workout! Have you ever experienced this?

In this financial empowerment process, there will be times when you feel like you can't go any further. There will be times that your own family and friends will make fun of you for the financial changes you have made or are trying to make. (By the way, if your broke family and friends are making fun of your financial plans, this means that you are doing something right!) Your Why is what will keep you going when things get tough. Your Why is going to drive you and keep you moving full steam ahead. Your Why has to be deep! For example, if you can find someone else that you are doing this for, such as your kids, loved ones, or family tree - make them a part of your Why. Doing so will move you to push beyond your limits, because you will not want to let them down. Thus, this journey becomes more than simply being about you not wanting to send the contents of your paycheck out of the door as soon as you get paid every two weeks; it becomes about building a life of security, stability and generational wealth for others!

If you refer back to my personal story, you will see that my Why was a combination of few things, which included positioning myself to be a future husband and leader of a household; retiring with dignity; powerfully impacting the community; and not following in the footsteps of my parents by making their same financial mistakes. What is your Why? It is your Why that is going to allow you to "live like no one else today, so later on you can live like no one else" as Dave Ramsey says. You have a choice: you can decide to keep living your life the same way that you are living today, financially burdened and having nothing to show for it, or you can decide that enough is enough and choose to pursue greatness by doing something different. The choice is entirely up to you. Whether you will choose one option or another is strongly contingent upon your ability to identify your Why. If your Why is compelling enough, nothing in the world stands a chance of stopping you from choosing to do something different.

When people embark upon a journey to financial freedom without first identifying their Why, their journey will be short lived. Believe it or not, everyone does not set out on this journey because of a strong conviction of Why it should be pursued; some people do it just because it's what everyone else seems to be doing – they're just giving it a try. Then, once they get started, they end up falling by the wayside when the going gets tough; when they get tired of putting in the work; or when they get worn out by all of the ongoing sacrifices that they need to make in order to become financially free. Without a clearly understood Why behind their actions, what they are doing can easily be compromised.

It is for this reason that it is imperative that you clearly understand your Why. Your Why will anchor you to your commitment more than you know, and it will keep you from throwing in the towel when you reach your wits' end. What you cannot do is give up during the process. You must keep pressing towards your goal, even when you get to the point that enough is enough – this is when doors start opening and opportunities start arising. International motivational speaker, Eric Thomas, put it best when he said, "Champions keep going when there is nothing left in their tank. When you find your why, you find a way to make it happen." So…what's your Why?

CHAPTER 5
What's Your Financial Kryptonite?

As much as we don't like to admit it, every single one of us has something in our life that serves as our "financial Kryptonite". The term kryptonite is derived from the story of the DC Comics superhero, "Superman". As you might know, Superman, considered the most powerful being on planet Earth, has a wide array of super powers which include, but are not limited to: superhuman strength; superhuman speed; flight; and x-ray vision. Combine that with an "S" on his chest, and it is obvious to see why he was my favorite superhero as a kid. Well, every superhero has a weakness, and Superman was no different. His ultimate weakness was kryptonite. As strong and powerful as Superman was, as soon as he was in the presence of kryptonite (the ore form of a radioactive element from Superman's home planet of Krypton), just being near it was enough to temporarily eliminate his powers. It left him feeling weak and depleted of energy; unable to fly, fight, or save the world. However, as soon as Superman could manage to get far enough away from the kryptonite, he was good to go; his powers were restored; and he could once again fly through the sky looking for someone to save.

You might be wondering, Why are we talking about Superman and kryptonite on our journey to financial freedom? I discuss this topic because it is something about which you will need to be aware on your financial journey. Almost everyone, including you, has a financial kryptonite: that one thing in our lives that we enjoy owning, doing, or participating in (whether we can afford it or not), that is derailing or has the potential to derail our financial progress. Much of the time, we are not even aware of the powerful force that our financial kryptonite has over our lives!

Everyone's kryptonite is different. For some, it's nights out on the town; for some it's shopping; for some it's having the latest and greatest technology; and for others it could be traveling. There are a variety of things that could serve as someone's kryptonite, causing them to completely blow their budget at the mere mention of one of these opportunities. The prospect of engaging in a particular behavior or having a certain thing or enjoying a particular experience makes them so weak that they simply cannot resist! It is for this reason that it is critical for you to identify your kryptonite. Without identifying your kryptonite, there is no way that you will ever be able to prosper financially. However, when you make an effort to figure out exactly what it is that can derail your financial empowerment process, you will know what your vulnerabilities are and maximize your chances of prospering financially by strengthening yourself at those vulnerable points.

As a former football player on both the high school and collegiate levels, I tend to use a lot of football analogies. Good football players know their weaknesses and they avoid getting caught in situations on the field that expose these vulnerable points. Good coaches help their player identify their weaknesses; once they are identified, the coach will not position his player in a place where his weakness can be exposed and taken advantage of by the opposing team.

I use this analogy to paint a picture of what is happening in our society today. We are not good players on the consumer playing field because our weaknesses have been exposed and broadcast to the world! For example, retailers, lenders, and auto dealers all know that one of the major weaknesses of mankind is impatience. It is human nature for us to want things immediately. Instantaneously. Right now! The thought of having to wait to get something is not acceptable to most people. Knowing this weakness of ours, retailers bombard us with new products every day, as well as new ways to buy these new products – even though we don't have the money.

Even more, retailers are masterful at appealing to our weaknesses of low self-concept and low self-image, making us feel like we are out of date if we do not have the latest version of whatever it is they have to offer. For this reason, most people will always seek to have the latest on-trend clothes; the latest shoes of the season; the newest mobile phone; and the latest fragrances; beauty products; hairstyles, etc. Rather than realize that we are financially tapped-out and cannot afford these luxuries, we always find a way to get them so that we can feel up to date and current. Our weaknesses have been exposed to the retail, lending, and auto industry, resulting in millions of debt-strapped consumers buying things that they can't afford every single day. Little do they know, but with each dollar that they spend on things that they cannot afford, they are throwing away their ability to build wealth.

Contentment: The Antidote to Kryptonite's

Derailing Power!

If you have identified your weakness, you now have the upper hand as you embark on this financial empowerment journey. However, there is another step that you must take as you prepare for the journey: being content. Contentment is defined as 'the state of satisfaction' or 'being satisfied with what one has'. Thus, while identifying your weakness is great, if you do not teach yourself to be happy with what you have at the moment, you will constantly be at war with yourself over the purchase of new things. Ultimately, you will fall right back into the habit of buying things that you cannot afford and derailing your financial goals. There is nothing wrong with wanting bigger, better, and nicer things; however the pursuit and acquisition of these things should not be the mission of your life. If you are given the opportunity to obtain these things that you want because you can financially afford them (i.e., you can purchase them without debt and without compromising your ability pay your other bills in any way), by all means capitalize on it and buy them!

My Kryptonite Story

It was in 2005 that I fell in love with the BMW M3 E46. I was playing the video game Need for Speed: Most Wanted, and I finally beat the game to have the car unlocked. For non-video game enthusiasts, when you beat the game, you "unlock" or gain access to the best car in the game, and this was the car that could easily destroy the competition! After one race, I smoked the competition so badly that I was able to cross the finish line in reverse! Okay, that didn't happen... but I still finished with a large margin of victory! It was this moment, as a college kid, that I decided that I was going to own this car someday.

The BMW M3 E46 was produced from 2001 to 2006. During its time, it was considered the best "bang for your buck" vehicle, in terms of having a super car performance at a $60,000 price tag. Car review magazines such as Car and Driver, Road and Track, and Motor Trend were salivating at the mouth about this car! The car produced 333 horsepower and went from zero to 60 in an amazing 4.7 seconds. It was a six cylinder, so it was also decent on gas, getting 16 miles per gallon in the city and 26 miles per gallon on the highway. As you can see, I did my research. I was so into this car!

Well, fast forward seven years later to June of 2012. I had been debt free for two years now, and I was able to really accumulate cash. I was saving on average about $1,000 a month while still living comfortably – experiencing the power of being financially empowered. I had saved about $22,000 in my savings account, which also included my emergency fund. It was around this time that I began looking to upgrade from my 2006 Honda Civic. I figured that I had worked hard for it, so I deserved it. Right? Excited about the potential of finally owning my dream car, I started looking at the M3's, of course.

After finding one in Chicago, I flew from Atlanta to the "Windy City" to check it out with high hopes of buying it; I didn't even have an airline ticket purchased for the return flight back home. After meeting up with Roy, the seller, at a local Wells Fargo Bank, and examining the car, I went ahead and made the purchase. We agreed on $18,500. I will never forget the look on his face when he realized that a 26 year old was handing him $10,000 cash and writing him a cashier's check in the amount of $8,500. It was priceless!

After purchasing the car, I began my 11-hour journey back to Atlanta, but only after eating some deep dish Chicago-style pizza, which has become my favorite type of pizza since that experience. And oh yeah... the drive back was a lot of fun too! Especially going through the mountains of Tennessee.

Once I arrived back in Atlanta, I began rebuilding my emergency fund. However, as soon as I started to accumulate some savings, repairs and maintenance for my BMW started to pop up. Roy had sold the car to me before the required Service II Routine Maintenance, which I'd had no clue about. Had I known about it, I would have knocked more off the price! To my surprise, such a service cost about $2,000. That was a price tag that I was definitely not used to, coming from driving a Honda Civic! In any case, because it was my dream car, I took it in to have the service done. I figured that once the car underwent this preventative maintenance appointment, it would be good to go; I wouldn't have to worry about spending anything else. Boy, was I wrong!

Once I took the car in for the service, they discovered that my alternator was bad - it could go out at any moment. That added an additional $1,600 to the bill. At this point, I began to get frustrated. However, I calmed down by convincing myself that this would be the last major expense for a while. Again, I was wrong!

About five months later, I noticed a thumping noise when I would shift at low speeds. Because I had already spent so much money on the car, I became nervous about the possible expense for repairs. I went in to get the car checked out by an M3 specialist. I soon learned that there were a multitude of parts on the car that were not designed to last long, and any of these parts could be involved in the clunking. Added to this, I was told that I needed to do some additional preventative maintenance. The total bill came out to be a bank account-shattering $5,000!

At this point, I was forced to take a hard, serious look at my situation. I began to think that if I were to spend any more money on this car, I would be an idiot; I had already literally poured my savings – $8,600 – into the upkeep of this car over the past seven months. I realized that there was no way that I could ever prosper financially if I had to deal with repairs like this on a yearly basis. How could I be an advocate of financial empowerment if I was constantly staying broke? Why was I putting myself through this? I mean, I had worked hard to put myself into a stable, secure financial position, and yet, here I was, stuck financially.

Over the course of only seven months, I had met my financial kryptonite, and it caused my once-empowered financial position to completely lose strength and become severely crippled. Since I didn't have an emergency fund anymore, I was in constant worry about the next emergency that could pop up. Would this car hold up and allow me to regroup and rebuild my emergency and savings accounts, or were the last seven months only a foreshadowing of the expensive challenges that I would face with the car in the years to come? For the first time in two years, I experienced the type of anxiety that had already become foreign to me, as someone who was living debt-free. As much as I loved the car, I began to debate about whether or not I should let it go. Through much prayer and counsel, I decided to sell the vehicle. I felt that this was the direction in which God was leading me, and if I wanted to prosper financially, I needed to follow His lead.

Getting Back into Position: Recovering from My Kryptonite!

Upon selling the vehicle, my financial situation roared back to full strength! I sold the car for $4,500 more than I paid for it, which helped to reduce the losses that I had suffered from all of the money I had poured into it. I took a little bit of the money to buy myself a vehicle whose maintenance was much friendlier on my pockets, while still being reliable. I was easily back to saving $1,000 to $1,500 a month. My bank account was exploding! I was also investing 15% of my income. Things were looking up!

It was not until later that I realized that the M3 was actually my financial kryptonite. It had been robbing me of my ability to succeed financially, and I didn't even realize it! Accepting the fact that my dream car was keeping me from achieving my life dreams was a sobering thought. However, it was also a confirmation to me that I had made the right decision to sell the car. In doing so, I was able to propel my finances back to where they needed to be and live a life of financial empowerment and freedom once again.

In fact, I became so financially empowered that I started to think about what career moves I wanted to make. It was at this time that I started developing my financial coaching practice, True Financial, to help others to become financially empowered. As I coach my clients, I share with them my own story of how my financial kryptonite almost took me out! I advise them of the importance of identifying their own kryptonite on their journey to financial empowerment and how not doing so could potentially derail all of the progress they make. Most of all, I share my first-hand knowledge about how this means that sometimes you have to let go of the things that you cherish, in order to place yourself in an empowered financial condition.

I will eventually get back into another M3 one day; it is still my dream car. However, when I get into it the next time, I will be in a much better place, and it will be just the right time!

CHAPTER 6
The Credit Score Myth – EXPOSED!

If you are like most people, you have constantly heard your whole life about how important it is to build yourself a good credit score. You have been told that without a good credit score, you will not prosper financially. You have also been told that without a credit history, life will be challenging for you. Now, what if I told you that all of that information was wrong and that you were misguided? Well, this is exactly what I am telling you!

In America, the credit score has become one of the most highly revered tools in the personal finance world. The drive for credit has become so ingrained into our society today that people are not as concerned about building wealth as they are about building their credit. People's every financial decision is based upon how it affects their FICO Score. Our society worships at the altar of the almighty FICO! Because of this, there is scarcely anywhere that you can go these days without hearing a mention of it. From catching references about it on catchy television commercials to hearing about it while you are opening an account with most service providers, it is inescapable; you will inevitably hear people mention that powerful four-letter acronym, FICO!

Despite the fact that there are literally tens of millions people who are struggling financially because they became ensnared in the trap of debt that resulted when they tried to build their credit scores, the credit score myth – the false belief that one must have credit or face a difficult life – abounds. In part, this myth persists because those who are in debt still continue to perpetuate the myth of the necessity of credit amongst their friends and family, encouraging them to sign up for debt so that they, too, can build their own credit scores. We must ask ourselves, "At what point did life without credit become unthinkable or impossible?"

Understanding FICO: Scoring Doesn't Equal "Winning"!

The FICO credit scoring system was created in the 1970s by Fair Isaac and Company. Its primary purpose is to determine the creditworthiness of a person. In other words, it provides a score that is indicative of how risky it is to lend a person money. The credit score is made up of the following components:

- 35% of your score is based on your debt history
- 30% is based on your debt level
- 15% is based on the length of time you've been in debt
- 10% is based on new debt
- 10% is based on the type of debt.

These percentages are based on the importance of the five categories for the general population. For some groups, the importance of these categories may vary. For example, people who have not been using credit for long will be factored differently than those with a longer credit history.

The FICO score is arguably one of the most misunderstood financial tools in personal finance. How so? Because, remember, the credit score is a financial tool that is derived from your borrowing habits. It has nothing to do with your ability to save, build wealth, or generate income. All it tells you is whether you are good at borrowing money and paying it back. Like it or not, your credit score is not an indicator of whether or not you are winning financially!

As Dave Ramsey says, "Your FICO score is an I-love-debt score." To build or maintain your score means that you have to stay in debt your entire life! However, when you are in debt, you will never truly prosper, because you are giving your money to someone else. Doing this over a 40-year period can literally cost you millions of dollars in building wealth! This is not a deep piece of logic here. If you go into debt and pay the bank hundreds of thousands and millions of dollars over the scope of your lifetime in order to maintain your FICO score, how are you going to build wealth?

Believe it or not, someone with a high credit score is more than likely going to be facing financial stress than someone without a credit score. Why? Because to maintain such a high score requires them to constantly be engaged in borrowing and making payments, thereby restricting their resources, which can result in financial stress. Banks consider someone with a high FICO score a good customer. Keep in mind that a 'good customer' is someone who brings you a lot of profits; profits come from interest that you pay in debt payments to the banker. That said, do you want to be a good customer of the bank? Another individual could have $30,000 in the bank, make $60,000 a year, and have a zero credit score; however, according to the FICO calculations, they would be a bad person to loan money to, because they have no credit history.

Individuals with a zero credit score do not borrow. This means that they pay cash for things, only buying them when they afford to do so. (My definition of "afford" is to be able to pay cash or write a check for the full amount of a purchase without having to compromise your ability to pay your bills on time; your lifestyle; or your ability to live.). These people tend to live without the financial stress that comes when people accumulate debt and are faced with paying on these accounts every month. Studies have also shown that people who don't have any debt tend to be happier than those who do. Happier people tend to perform better at work; have better relationships; and tend to have increased spirituality. There are clear benefits to living the debt-free life – benefits that reach far beyond that of finances!

If you are running around trying to build your FICO score and you call this "winning with money", I hate to disappoint you, but you are sorely misinformed. You are not winning by taking on more debt! You are not even winning at proving that you can pay bills! The only thing that you are winning at, is proving that you love debt and plan to stay in it.

You, Yes YOU, Can Live without a Credit Score!

You might have a difficult time believing this, but you can, indeed, live without a credit score! You are not required to finance the purchases that you make throughout life, as so many would have you to believe. You can buy cars with cash, so there is no need to be concerned with getting a good interest rate. You can rent a house and open various service accounts, such as a mobile phone account, without having a credit score. Doing so might simply require you to put down a larger deposit; however, this is completely fine, because once you aren't making debt payments anymore, you will have more than enough cash for a deposit, which you will eventually get back!

You can also buy a home without credit. This tends to be people's biggest concern. Buying a home without credit just requires you to go through what they call "manual underwriting". Manual underwriting is when a mortgage company manually reviews your financial position and history instead of basing its decision on a credit score.

Additionally, you can also obtain employment without a credit score. If an employer will not hire you because you don't have a credit score, you do not need to work there. You are more than just a number; you are a human being of worth, with morals, values and character!

As you embark on your journey to financial freedom, do not buy into the myth that your credit score is the be-all and end-all. Trying to build and maintain your credit score has done nothing but left you stressed out, broke, and feeling like you are never going to prosper. Considering this, why not try something different? Why not view and handle your personal finances from a different perspective? One definition of insanity is to do the same thing over and over again, expecting different results each time. As you embark upon your financial empowerment journey, be prepared to do something different; rather than accumulating and managing debt - let's focus on eliminating debt, saving, and paying cash. Allow your goal to be having money, not having a high credit score. If you do so, you will be on your way to building some serious wealth!

Coach's Note

Forbes Magazine produces an annual issue dedicated to the 400 wealthiest people in America. When asked "What is the number one key for people to build wealth?" an overwhelming majority of 75% responded "To become debt-free and stay debt-free". Wealthy people understand the power of being free and not chained to debt. It is said that a smart man learns from his own experiences, but a wise man learns from the experiences of others. Follow the lead of those who have attained the levels of wealth that you desire to attain. The sooner you can free up your income by getting out of debt, the sooner you can begin to build wealth. Don't waste time; start building wealth now!

CHAPTER 7
The Final Step before the Official Journey: Detoxing with a Financial Fast!

You have undoubtedly learned quite a bit about yourself in the last few chapters, and I am sure that you are ready to get this show on the road and set your wheels in motion to speed off on your journey towards financial empowerment. However, there's one more thing – and it's an important one. Do you remember our little chat about how personal finance is less about math than it is about behavior? I hope so, because that understanding will be critical in your ability to embrace the need for this final step on your journey!

There are plenty of people who earn $200,000 a year and yet live from paycheck to paycheck. On the other hand, there are those who make $50,000 a year, live comfortably, invest, and have a fully-funded emergency fund. What's the differentiating factor here? It's their behavior! Regardless of how much money you make, you will never be able to begin building wealth if you always allow your behavior to get in the way. The way you think about and relate to money will always sink your best wealth-building efforts faster than a cannonball can sink a ship! It's time to resolve once and for all not to allow your behaviors to sink your financial ship, and it's time to put some real action to that resolve!

Now, just as you are officially setting out on your financial journey, is the moment when you will begin what I call a "financial fast". Like any other fast you might have tried, that altered your food consumption, this financial fast will alter your financial consumption! In general, fasts help us to break habits of unhealthy eating that we have engaged in for years. Along the way, our dietary fasts help to detoxify our bodies and reset our systems so that we can start living with new eating habits after the fast is over. So it will go with the financial fast. During this time, you will restrict or go without spending money on certain things that you have habitually spent money on for years. In fact, spending money on them is as natural as breathing air; you don't even think about them… but now you will! You will need to do the financial fast in tandem with Power Move 1 (the next chapter), because it will help you as you create a budget that will guide your income during your journey.

Just like a dietary fast, your financial fast will be challenging when you first begin, and you will definitely want to cheat or quit on it in the same way you want to just throw in the towel and grab a greasy cheeseburger and some hot French fries during a fast from food. However, you must continue to remind yourself that what you have been doing for so many years has not been working; it's time to do something different in order to realize different results. Think about it - the financial habits that you have been engaging in for the past several years are doing nothing to help you get you the results that you want. Therefore, in order to get rid of them and build a new foundation with healthy financial behaviors, you will need to begin the process by first "shocking" your financial system through this one month fast.

The financial fast operates like this… For one entire month, you will do only the minimum amount of spending with your money, by spending money only on essential necessities such as groceries, rent, gas, insurance, utilities, and other goods necessary for basic survival. NO money is to be spent on luxuries such as going to clubs (unless it's the Boys and Girls Club); movies (watch one on television or read a book instead); restaurants (yes, you will have to cook, even on date night); or clothes and shoes (since you're not going out, put that new pair of shoes down and back away from the store)! Don't worry, it's not the end of the world! You can still have a great time on your financial fast if you just tap into your creativity. For example, find free things to do like going to the park, going on a bike ride, going hiking or taking advantage of the various free local events in your city.

Your financial fast plays a powerful role in helping to advance your efforts towards a wealth-building future, because it promises to do the following: 1) It will teach you that it doesn't cost you as much to live as you think; 2) It will help you to identify the habits that are "nickel and diming" away your ability to be powerful financially; 3) It will teach you to appreciate the luxuries in your life while also realizing they are not necessities; and 4) It will allow you to just slow down, which tends to help people figure out what is really important in their lives.

To date, I have successfully led more than 500 people through this fast; and I can assure you that you too, will have tremendous success! Before you are even midway through the fast, you will have quickly begun to identify the habits that were keeping you broke. You will also, more than likely, have more money in your bank account because you are no longer spending it all, just because it is there for you to spend. I'm telling you - this financial fast will change your entire perspective on things!

Beth, a past financial fast participant, said, "I learned so much about myself during the fast! I used to swipe my debit card every day without thinking, and then I would wonder where all of my money went! Since I purposely did not do that for one month, I really saw a difference. I've also taken time to notice the blessings in my life! For my birthday, I was given a gift card to a restaurant, which made a great free lunch for my family one day during the fast. I used a code for a free movie rental, which was another great family activity that was FREE! No money spent, and I still enjoyed life! I am so grateful for the great learning opportunity that the financial fast has offered me!"

As wonderful as the financial fast will turn out to be in your life, be prepared for the opposition, for they will come along dangling "can't miss" outings and "amazing" opportunities before your eyes that will seem as enticing on your financial fast as a big, moist piece of chocolate cake would be on a dietary fast! This is where your firm resolve and will power must kick in; remember your Why, and simply reply with "No, thanks. I'm good!" Your friends will constantly challenge the notion of your saying "No"; during your fast, it will seem like you are probably turning down more invitations to hang out with them and spend money than ever before. As a result, they will question what you are doing. They might even begin to question your sanity! However, do not worry; you are doing this for you. You are doing this for the betterment of your future.

Another past client, Joshua, had this to say about his friends during his financial fast: "So we were not even an entire week into the fast, and the first week brought on some turbulent conversations about why I was doing this "financial fast"! My friends would make comments like, 'Student loan debt is good debt!' and 'Being in debt is needed to build credit!' They would also ask questions like, 'Why can't you go out with us? Are you just being cheap?' It was frustrating, because I didn't expect this from certain people! However, each interaction was greeted with a smile, because I knew that this financial boost would guide the rest of my year, if I would let it. Although there was no one keeping me accountable every single minute of the day, being more conscious about spending, during and after this process, was one of my many great takeaways from the financial fast."

From the testimonies of these clients, you can clearly see that though this fast will definitely challenge you, the rewards are certain, and the changed perspective that it will leave you with, as you begin to build wealth, is priceless. You can survive the financial fast like so many others have, using it as a springboard to launch them into their journey to financial empowerment! Confucius, the wise Chinese philosopher, once said, "The man who says he can and the man who says he cannot are both correct." If you think you can do it, then you will, so get your mind right as you prepare to help yourself become financially empowered, starting with the fast!

Want to "Amp Up" the Financial Fast Challenge?

Maximize Your Fast by Connecting with Your CASH!

Some people – usually adventurers, the super-competitive, thrill seekers, and those who love a good challenge – are always in search of ways to take things to the next level. As a fast car lover and speed enthusiast myself, I can relate! If you are this kind of person, I've got a challenge for you: if you really want to take your financial fast to another level, increase the difficulty of it by putting the debit and credit cards away and only using cash throughout the duration of the fast!

One of the major problems with our current society is that we do not use cash anymore. Before the common use of debit and credit cards, people simply used cash. Numerous studies have shown that people spend more money when they make purchases using debit and credit cards. Why? Because when you use a card, the transaction is just a bunch of numbers! For example, McDonalds only began to accept credit and debit cards after they conducted a study that showed that when consumers bought food using their debit and credit cards, the average sale went from $4.75 to $7 per order. People were likely to spend 47% more when they could pay with their card! Of course, in light of this discovery, McDonald's immediately decided to accept credit cards, regardless of the processing fees charged to them by card companies such as Visa, Master Card, American Express and Discover.

There is a reason why we spend less when we have to reach into our wallets and fork over cash to buy something: we have an emotional connection to our cash; because it actually represents all of the time, energy, and work that we invested into earning it. We see it as our "hard earned" money for a reason, and something that we have worked so hard to earn is in no way easy to give away. To see it leaving us and going to the cashier as we physically hand it over for a purchase, causes us to feel an emotional tug as the bills and coins leave our hand. If you accept the challenge to only spend cash during your financial fast, it will make you think a lot more about the hours that you worked to earn that income, and as a result, you will spend less!

In the Sample Budget that is included in the Appendix, you will see the icon of an envelope next to certain budget categories. This envelope icon is present to recommend that you use cash for these particular budget categories, which generally include groceries, restaurants, clothing, car repairs, entertainment, etc.

Additionally, to make it easier for you to keep up with your money, I suggest using actual envelopes to organize your cash. Place the cash that you will need for each budget category into a separate envelope and then mark the budget category on the front. For example, you would create an envelope marked "Groceries" and then put the amount of cash that is allotted for groceries into that budget.

If you get paid bi-weekly, then you would place half of the monthly budget into the envelope on the first payday of the month and the second half on the second pay of the month. For example if your grocery budget is $700, then $350 would be placed in the envelope on the first pay day of the month and another $350 would be added to the envelope on the second pay day of the month.

For other budget categories - when you place the cash into their respective envelopes will depend on how your income flows. If you get paid once a month, you would place the entire amount for each budget category into its proper envelope. If you are paid weekly, you might need to split up the budget amounts into four different installments. For example, if you are paid on a weekly basis and your grocery budget is $700, you would place $187.50 per pay check into the envelope marked "Groceries" each week.

Now that you have "gotten your head right" and committed to your financial fast (some of you having accepted the additional challenge of only using cash along the way) for the next 30 days, it's time to officially set out on the journey by stepping into our first Power Move! Ready, set, go!

Power Move 1:
Plan, then Command Your Money!

Welcome to the first Power Move! The first Power Move is the most important of all, because each of the other Power Moves stems from this first step. In fact, without this first Power Move, the others are not even possible!

Right now, you probably govern your financial life like most Americans: you kind of have an idea of where your money is going – but not really. You get paid, and then you pay all of your bills. Whatever is left after you pay bills, is what you consider to be your discretionary money – money you can spend on things that you want, however you like. This is how the majority of Americans handle their money. Rather than be proactive with our money, we tend to be reactive with it.

Dr. Stephen Covey says in his book, The 7 Habits of Highly Effective People, that the number one habit of highly effective people is that they are proactive. This means that they happen to life as opposed to simply allowing life to happen to them. They make an impact on the life that is going on around them. Regardless of what happens in their lives, they do not use victim language, positioning themselves as helpless recipients of what life has thrown at them. Instead, they consider themselves to possess the power and ability to change things in their lives for the better and to transform whatever negative circumstances they encounter into positive ones that work for their benefit. They actively make a dent in things instead of passively waiting for things make a dent in them. This is exactly how you will need to be with your finances if you want to prosper financially.

Being proactive is directly tied to being intentional. When you are intentional about managing your money, you won't have random dollars escaping from your bank account every month. In addition to positively impacting your bank account, being intentional has also been proven to positively impact every other area of your life; money touches, influences, and impacts every other part of your personal existence. The relationship between your money and your personal life is the very reason that it's called 'personal finance'!

Establish the Plan (aka The Dreaded B-word!)

The very first proactive and intentional step that you must take, is to establish the plan - a budget. If the muscles in your shoulders just tensed up and your heart just raced a little faster with anxiety upon reading the word "budget", you are not alone. Because of the free-spending society in which we live, the word "budget" has become a serious taboo. People simply do not like the thought of something dictating to them what they can spend and when they can spend it. Instead, they would rather continue living like they have always lived – by the seat of their pants, buying what they want instead of spending on what they need; financing their purchases if they do not have the money, and finding a way to stay afloat every month – without having to answer to anyone, or anything, for their unrestricted and undisciplined behaviors.

People in our society have been conditioned to dislike the term "budget". At the mere mention of the word, they cringe as if they are about to get rid of cable, be forced to eat Ramen Noodles, and see all of the fun drain hopelessly out of their lives. I personally believe that this widely-held perspective of what "budget" connotes, stems from experiences in our careers; with the government; and with our parents. When we heard the phrase, "It's not in the budget," this meant that they could not afford to purchase something. In other words, it is simply another way of saying, "No! You can't have it!" – and no one likes to hear a "No". We have equated "budget" with denial of access to things; thus, we have developed a negative view of what "budget" means.

What's more, whenever we hear the topic of a budget discussed on the news, it is always in a negative light. All we tend to hear about on the news surrounding budgets, are budget cuts, which equate to job loss, or governmental stand-stills among Washington D.C. lawmakers, because they can't mutually agree on a budget. Each time we see incidences like these in the media, we absorb a little more negativity about what "budget" means; inevitably, we apply this meaning to our own lives, and the result is that we tend to view budgets negatively. The truth of the matter is that while we tend to associate a budget with being restrictive or causing lack in our lives, in actuality, a budget is just a plan of what you expect to do with your earned income for a certain period of time.

The best way to be proactive, is to create a monthly budget before you get your income for the month. If you wait until after you have received your income, to make your budget, you will find that you discover plenty of ways to spend your money throughout the month; without a laid out plan for your money, by the end of the month, you will inevitably have more month than you have money. Thus, it is necessary to be proactive with your money by budgeting, or else your money will leave, without you having any idea of where it went. From this day forward, think of your budget as your personal plan that is designed to help you take care of the resources in your possession and to help you build wealth.

How to Create a Budget

To create a budget, start out by listing each and every bill payment, debt, and financial obligation that you have. Include debts such as student loans, credit cards, and car payments; these need to be addressed aggressively, because they result in "paycheck to paycheck living".

There is one special consideration that I will ask you to make, as you are making your budget. You might already be doing some investing, sending a certain amount of your money each month into a mutual fund, an IRA, a 529, etc. However, at this point on your journey, I recommend that you temporarily stop investing. You are about to embark on a debt reduction plan, and this will require freeing up as much income as possible, so that it can go towards your debt. This might seem like an odd or unconventional request, but trust me! As humans, the power of focus is huge for us; being able to focus everything you can on eliminating your debt will help you to achieve much better results much sooner than investing and engaging in debt elimination at the same time. Think of the power of focus this way. Light diffused through a light bulb is focused in many different directions so that it can light up a room. However, when you take that same light and route it through a high power laser, the intensity of the focused energy can literally cut through a wall! The power of focus can do much damage! Thus, I encourage you to not have your income spread out in many different directions. Instead, focus it in the here and now on eliminating your debt. Later, you can focus that same income on investing. Once you put a temporary halt on your investment activities, include the money as income in your budget planning.

For greater detail on the type of budget that you will create, consider whether you will create an open-ended budget or a zero-based budget and follow the guidelines for the development of the type you prefer.

An Open-Ended Budget vs. a Zero-Based Budget: Which is Best?

The mere thought of preparing a budget can be intimidating for you if you are new to the world of responsibly managing your personal finances and have never done a budget before. If you have developed a written budget before and failed at it, or if you have very loosely created a budget in your mind in the past and found yourself unable to stick to it, approaching the task of developing a budget again can be particularly daunting. You don't want to fail again at sticking to your budget, and that is understandable.

Over years of coaching clients on their journey to financial empowerment, I have discovered that one of the primary reasons that people fail at being able to stick to their budgets, is because they use an open-ended budget; these are, quite frankly, really difficult to stick to. An open-ended budget is one that does not place every single dollar you earn into a particular category. As a result, you end up having unassigned and uncommitted money that somehow is magically spent by the end of the month.

The opposite of the open-ended budget is the zero-based budget. This is the type of budget that I recommend. A zero-based budget starts out with your income listed at the top of the page, and it assigns every single dollar into to a particular category. When you get to the bottom of the page, you should have zero dollars left. The zero does not mean that every dollar will be spent; it just indicates that every dollar is appropriately accounted for in a designated category – hence, the name "zero-based budget". You can see an example of a zero-based budget in the Appendix.

Note: As an added bonus for purchasing this book, you can download the Monthly Cash Flow Plan by visiting
www.truefinancialcoaches.com.

Budgeting for the Single Person: Don't Go At It Alone!

Being single has a lot of pros when it comes to budgeting. The good thing is that because you are single, you do not have to answer to anyone but yourself on matters pertaining to your budget. The bad thing is that you do not have to answer to anyone but yourself on matters pertaining to your budget!

Creating a budget as a single person is great; it's easier and less complex because you can lay out your plan without having to factor in anyone else's input. It is truly YOUR budget! However, the downside to that is that you have to hold yourself accountable. There is no one there to look over your shoulder and question you when you start to veer away from your budget plan. Therefore, as easy as it was to create the budget, it can be just as easy to overspend or discard the budget entirely.

Accountability is a key success factor in getting things done. Research shows that greater levels of accountability correspond to greater levels of success, because when we have to answer to someone else for our attitudes or behaviors, we are more likely to be aware of engaging in the right ones, which will lead to achieving a desired outcome. After all, who wants to report back to our accountability partners that we have been undisciplined, irresponsible, rebellious against the plan that we have laid out for ourselves? However, when we have no accountability and know that we will not have to answer to anyone else for our attitudes and behaviors, we are prone to engage in behaviors that would otherwise be questioned – behaviors that will not lead us to our desired outcome.

If you are single, I highly recommend that, rather than going at the budgeting process alone, you find a friend or family member that you trust to be a good accountability partner. A good accountability partner will help to keep you in check when you are having a moment of weakness or when you have just been slacking with your budgeting. For example, a good accountability partner would be someone who is financially responsible and who is either empowered or working towards being empowered, in his or her own finances. This is a person who is not afraid to question you about your spending decisions and one who will not back down, even if you kick, yell, scream, and pout about wanting to spend your hard-earned money the way you want. Regardless of how resistant you are, they will hold you accountable to your budget. On the other hand, I would not recommend choosing your spend-happy shopping buddy to be your accountability partner; when you are considering overspending, your "buddy" will encourage you to buy ten shirts instead of talking you out of this purchase that will blow your budget! The person whom you select as your accountability partner is going to be key to helping you to achieve financial success, so choose carefully!

Budgeting with a Spouse: You've Got to Play by the Rules!

If you are married, more than likely one spouse in the household manages the family's finances because he or she is better at it. Whoever you choose to handle the finances in the relationship is completely up to you - just make sure that it is the best choice for maintaining a healthy financial condition. Also, while one partner will be primarily responsible for managing the household's finances, this does not exclude the other from the responsibility of working with that partner in making critical financial decisions. Remember, you are partners on the same team, so both of your inputs matter! As we learned in the financial personality chapter, when both spouses work together on the household finances, the relationship tends to improve drastically. This is due, in large part, to the fact that the channels of communication tend to open up more, allowing the spouses to engage in dialogue to understand one another.

Budgeting with your spouse will not always be comfortable; being able to develop and maintain a commitment to your household budget will require both you and your spouse to step out of your respective comfort zones. Despite the challenging nature of working with another person – often a very different one – on a budget plan, it is through those challenges that you will find success; and we all desire to be successful when it comes to money.

When preparing to have your budget meeting with your spouse, consider the time and surroundings, because these have an impact on the atmosphere in which you will be discussing an already sensitive, delicate, and potentially volatile subject. This initial budget meeting will be the most difficult and usually the longest (subsequent monthly meetings won't be anything like the first one), so you will want to do all you can to ensure that you and your partner meet at a time and location in which you are both as relaxed and at ease as possible. Meet at a time that is best for both of your schedules, and before setting a meeting time, ask your spouse if the time works for them – do not just assume that it does! If you have children, you might want to wait until the children have gone to school or wait until they have gone to bed for the night. Regarding location, I would suggest holding the meeting in an area of the house that is comfortable for the both of you and well lit. Some people choose to use the dining room table, while others prefer a more relaxed area like the living or family room. Then again, you could always choose to have your budget meeting away from the house on a "date night" or at a coffee house. I tend to recommend the off-site locations for budget meetings that occur once you become debt-free. You are trying to save money, after all!

Take note that this is only the first of many monthly budget meetings. Monthly budget meetings are for reporting, accountability, and maintenance. They should not take a long time, and for the most part, they should be quick and painless. However, as you are getting started on your budgeting journey, there will also be a need to call "emergency budget meetings" with your spouse. These will be held between your monthly budget meetings, to address critical issues that are compromising the functionality of the budget that you established together. Let's face it, you are new to budgeting, so things will more than likely be forgotten off the budget, understated, and even overstated. For example, one common thing that people tend to forget, are the irregular expenses that pop up every now and then – things like going to the dentist or visiting the doctor. Then, groceries have a tendency to be either over or understated, because the price of groceries can fluctuate depending on whether you buy lots of items on sale or not. For best results, I always encourage my clients to try this fun challenge while they are working to get out of debt: build your grocery list using only the items that are on sale, and then see what fun recipes you can create using them!

The first step to approaching the development of a budget plan with your spouse is calling an initial household budget meeting. When having the household budget meeting, each personality type will need to abide by certain rules in order for the meeting to be productive and effective.

Household Budget Meeting Rules for "The Nerd"

In order for the monthly household budget meeting to be productive for the Nerd, he or she will need to come to the budget meeting with the budget already drafted (assuming that the Nerd is married to a Free Spirit, which typically is the case). Let's face it, the last thing that a Free Spirit wants to do is to go to a budget meeting. Free Spirits would rather be running through a field with the wind blowing in their hair or doing the wave in a packed sports stadium; thus, having a budget already drafted will cut down on the length of the meeting and the pain and misery that the Free Spirit will have to endure sitting through it.

The second thing that the Nerd must do is LISTEN! Nerds tend to think that they are always right, especially when it comes to something like performing precise calculations on a budget, so they will assume that their budget is perfect. Therefore, when they arrive at a budget meeting, it is usually to talk – to disseminate information on the things that the household needs to do, the rules for doing them, and the consequences for not following the rules. For them, the fact that the gathering is called a "meeting" is a mere formality, because they have little interest in hearing the Free Spirit's input on the matter. It is for this reason that the Nerd must be deliberately intentional about listening!

The third rule for the Nerd complements the second one: BE QUIET while listening to your spouse, as he or she provides input! Your spouse can talk as long as he or she wants – as long as it takes to work through the three to five changes in the budget that are necessary. If you, the Nerd, interrupt, you will be sending the message to your spouse that his or her opinion does not matter, and it will discourage your spouse from making any real, meaningful contributions from that point on.

Finally, the Nerd must remember to keep the budget meeting brief. This should not be an all-day family retreat! Work as long as it takes for both of you to have your say, come to a win-win resolve, and then wrap up the meeting!

Household Budget Meeting Rules for "The Free Spirit"

In order for the monthly household budget meeting to be productive for the Free Spirit, the Free Spirit will need to actually show up for the meeting! I know how difficult this can be for the Free Spirit, but believe me when I tell you: showing up is literally half of the battle for a person with this financial personality! The last thing that a Free Spirit wants to do is go to a meeting where they are setting up "restrictions" for themselves. If Free-Spirits instead look at the budget meeting as a time to create a plan that will allow them to live their Free Spirit ways, while effectively achieving their goals, they win! Thus, you must be careful to pitch the idea of a meeting to the Free Spirit in the right way!

The second thing that the Free Spirit will need to do, is provide input for the budget. Free Spirits are notorious for foregoing the opportunity to provide any input or feedback on the budget, instead making dismissive statements like, "Do whatever you feel like honey," or "I trust that you'll do what's best for our family," or "I don't care"! However, taking this route is a cop out! I always challenge every married Free Spirit client that I have, to make at least three to five changes to the budget that their Nerd spouses have put together. I do this because I recognize that in order for the budget to have any kind of value to the Free Spirit, he or she must contribute to the budget's creation.

Finally, the Free Spirit needs to be realistic when providing input on the budget. For example, for a Free Spirit to say that the grocery budget should be cut to just $100 a month is not realistic; you will not be able feed a household on such a small amount of money. Therefore, the Free Spirit must come to the meeting ready to think through things, analyze, and calculate – as painful a proposition as this might be. Consider it this way: becoming engaged at this level for only fifteen minutes or so, during the meeting, is a small price to pay for helping your spouse to have a greater level of appreciation for your judgment. Best of all, taking time to realistically think about the three to five things that you will provide input on will leave you with the feeling of being invested in the budget and of doing your part towards helping your family to become financially empowered!

Living with a Budget Plan is a Marathon, Not a Sprint!

When you create a budget plan, do not expect your budget to work perfectly your first time through. In fact, it will take you about three to four months of solid budgeting to get it down. Over time, you will see the results of sticking to your budget, and there will be measurable results to indicate that your plan is working. Regardless of how rough things get, be committed to staying in the race; budgeting is a long-term marathon, not a short-term sprint.

Budgeting is just like learning how to ride a bicycle. You do not just hop on a bicycle for the very first time and instantly become an X-Games professional! Instead, the first several times you hop onto the seat, you will fall off the bicycle. There will be bumps, bruises, and scrapes along the way, but as long as you keep getting back on, you will very soon be riding along easily and smoothly!

The same applies to how you can expect your budget planning process to go. Though you have firmly established the budget and have every intention of sticking to it, everything will not go smoothly in the beginning. You might find that you forgot to include something in the budget; that emergency budget meetings need to be called because an unexpected expense popped up; that the budget was simply unrealistic; or that overspending occurred in one area, which requires adjustments to be made in other areas. In any case, despite the hiccups that you encounter along the way, maintain your commitment to developing and sticking to your monthly budget! After several months of practice, I assure you that things will get easier, and you'll be gliding along like a pro!

Got a Budget Plan? Now It's Time to "Command" Your Money!

Congratulations on establishing your budget plan! Now that you have a plan for how your money will be allocated each month, the next step is to command your money. I use the term "command" your money very strategically. You see, most people are reactive to their money and govern their behavior based upon what their money says that they can do. However, to "command your money" is to take a proactive approach in which you tell your money what to do instead. You issue the orders, not your money!

Your very first priority is to quickly save $1,000 if you make more than $20,000 a year or $500 if you make less than $20,000 a year. This money will serve as your "starter emergency fund"; later, during Power Move 3, you will fully fund your emergency fund, which will be equivalent to the amount of three to six-months' worth of your living expenses. For now, however, $1,000 should cover the cost of any typical emergencies that might pop up, such as an insurance deductible for a car accident, a home repair, an auto repair, etc.

It is very important that you place a barrier between yourself and a potential disaster. Not having an emergency fund is the easiest way to ensure that you will remain broke and in debt for the rest of your life. Life will inevitably happen, and without access to emergency funds, you will simply end up digging a bigger hole of debt for yourself in order to deal with it. If you just take a few moments to reflect on how many times "life" has already happened to you, you will realize the truth of this notion.

If life operates at any level according to Murphy's Law, what can go wrong will go wrong. I like to add a caveat to this: wrong things tend to happen much more when you do not have an emergency fund in place. Thus, it is critical that you establish your starter emergency fund at the beginning, even before you begin to pay down your debt! The last thing that you need as you try to pay off your debt, is to face a situation in which you have to take on more debt to address an emergency – an emergency that could have easily been addressed with less than $1,000. See-sawing back and forth between making progress in paying off debt while having to take on more debt to survive an emergency, is a fast way to get de-motivated. Bad things happen to those who don't prepare, so my advice to you is to get prepared!

Power Move 2:

Get Your Snowball on a Roll!

Now that you have established a budget plan and commanded your money to the tune of saving $500 to $1,000 in an emergency starter fund, it is time to attack your debt head-on! Unfortunately, many people have bought into the notion that being in debt is simply a way of life and that living debt-free is not a realistic way to live. As a result, they lack the confidence that they can ever pay down their debt and become debt-free. However, with a plan, resolve, and commitment to launch a full-frontal attack on eliminating debt from your life, it can be done!

Part of the reason that so many people do not confront their debt or ever attempt to pay it down, is that they simply do not know how. Unfortunately, society has done a great job teaching us how to get into debt, but it offers little to no instruction on how to get out of it. When you think about it, for this to be the case makes perfect sense. We live in a society that is driven by borrowing. In fact, economists gauge how well the economy is doing based upon the level of borrowing activity by consumers and investors.

For people to be taught how to pay off debt would be contradictory to the debt-driven economy and society that we live in today!

For most people, the mountain of debt that they have amassed over the years looms so large and ominous before them, that to even think about paying off their debt seems as impossible as climbing Mount Everest in a snowstorm. However, when people are equipped with easy-to-understand information and methods that they can apply to their debt-reduction efforts in a practical manner, the confidence that they need to attack their debt increases, they are able to envision living debt-free lives, and they are motivated to "get on a roll" to get it done! In this chapter, I will equip you with a proven methodology that I have used time and again with my clients to help them do what many consider to be impossible: become completely debt free – and much sooner than they ever thought possible!

When Working to Reduce Debt, Attitude is

EVERYTHING!

If you recall, we discussed at-length the importance of knowing your "Why?" before embarking on this road to financial empowerment. We have now reached the point at which your understanding of your "Why?" is especially critical: it will play a key role in the attitude that you have as you undertake this journey!

You see, Power Move 2 is a challenging Power Move, because it requires you to change your behavior and lifestyle. It requires you to cut back on your spending in order to maximize your debt elimination power. It is going to require you to delay pleasure in the here and now in order to obtain future gratification. For example, Power Move 2 will require you to minimize how frequently you eat out at restaurants. In fact, in this phase of your journey, you shouldn't be in a restaurant unless you work there. This Power Move will require you to minimize and all but eliminate spur-of-the-moment purchases. As for vacations, they will be pretty much non-existent. If these seem like radical adjustments, there is good reason: drastic financial times call for drastic financial measures!

Think about it: you have created a financial mess for yourself. Do you really think that spending money on something like a vacation makes good financial sense? Taking a vacation away from your financial mess is counterproductive, because that same money could be used to get you out of debt and move you towards achieving financial freedom that much sooner. This is not to say that you will never be able to take a vacation again; it is to say that now is not the time nor the financial season to do so. Thus, your vacation and other financial splurges are not completely denied; they are merely delayed until you have a better control of your finances.

Dave Ramsey is noted for saying, "Children do what feels good. Adults devise a plan and stick to it," and his words could not be more correct! The truth is that delaying gratification is already difficult enough for us as human beings; when you combine it with how the microwave society in which we currently live, shapes our appetites, the level of difficulty is dramatically increased! In order to overcome the demands of your appetite to have things "right now" and be willing to defer the gratification for those things, you must approach this process with focused intentionality. Human beings can achieve great things through the power of focus! In this case, when the sacrifices you are required to make seem to become too overwhelming, be sure to keep your focus on your "Why?"

Another key reason that you must navigate this journey with your "Why?" in full view, is that inevitably, people are going to view you as different or weird as you go through your process. However, do not be discouraged - this is perfectly fine! When this begins to occur, just know that you are doing something right. In our society, what is normal is being broke; what is different or abnormal is striving to be debt-free. Thus, being weird and different is where you want to be! Just be prepared for your normal, broke friends to make fun of you and make statements like, "You need to enjoy life, because life is too short to live like that!" To that statement you should reply, "Life is too short to spend it in debt and being oppressed!" Then, keep on moving with your "Why?" in clear focus ahead of you!

With focused intensity, getting out of debt should not take you ten years; it should move much more quickly than this. After all, one can only be focused for so long. As you go along, keep in mind that the amount of time for which you will have to delay gratification of the things you really want, is a relatively short period of time in comparison to the whole span of your life. Therefore, get it over with now! If you do, you can spend the rest of your years enjoying an empowered life, doing the things that you want to do, and paying cash for them!

Don't Waste Your Time:

Debt-Reduction Methods that Don't Really Work

Before we dive into my professional recommendation for the best method for being able to quickly and effectively pay off your debt, let's first address the most common methods that people use to pay off debts – methods that do not really work for most people.

The first approach that most people take towards paying off debt is that of paying off their debt with the highest interest rate first, the second-highest interest rate next, and so on, all the way down to the debt with the lowest interest rates. Mathematically, this approach makes sense; paying the debt with the highest interest rate first would actually save you money in the amount of interest that you would pay back. Unfortunately, this approach does not seem to work for most people for one essential reason: they are not required to make any real adjustments in their behavior. As a result, they just stay in debt, never making any real progress.

As we learned earlier, personal finance is about behavior. In light of this fact, in order to be effective in your debt-reduction efforts, you have to address your debt in a way such that your personal financial behavior is modified. This approach of paying off debt in order of highest-to-lowest interest rates calls for no real modification in debt-paying behavior. Also, because the goal is to quickly eliminate your outstanding debt, the amount of interest paid is minimized to the point where it is irrelevant. Interestingly enough, if someone paid off his debt using the highest-to-lowest interest rate approach, not implementing our teachings, they would more than likely pay more interest.

It is important to understand here that the high interest rates are not the issue; the interest rates are not why you are in debt! You are in debt because of the choices that you made, which influenced your spending behavior. People who take the approach of paying off debts with the highest interest rates first, tend to grow discouraged and never finish their debt elimination plans because they never experience the quick wins that paying the smallest debt first, and then the next smallest, and so on, offer to them – and these small wins are more important than you realize! Winning is huge for humans, because we are a competitive species. When you are trying to eliminate debt and are not experiencing wins (like accounts being labelled as "paid-off" and "closed"), you tend to easily grow discouraged and abort the process. I liken this method to an example of how we try to lose weight. If your trainer told you that you would have to work out for 20 weeks and then your results would instantly appear, it would be hard to stay committed to your diet and exercise plan. However, if you see yourself making gradual, incremental progress along the way, these results help you to stay motivated so that you will keep going, striving to achieve even better results, and eventually hit your target!

Another method of paying off debt that is a waste of time, is debt consolidation. In debt consolidation, a person combines multiple debts into just one debt – thus, "consolidating" them – usually offered at a lower interest rate than the original debts themselves. While this method might appear attractive on the surface, debt consolidation is ineffective for a number of reasons.

First, debt consolidation only treats the symptoms of the behaviors that got you into debt. Larry Burkett, noted financial author, says that debt is not the problem; it is the symptom. Debt is a symptom of overspending, and it is indicative of people's belief that they need to go into debt in order to attain the things they want in life. The only thing that debt consolidation does is move your money from one holder of your debt to another, and debt consolidation companies charge you fees to do so. Moving your debt around from place to place won't help you find your way out of debt; the only way to get out of debt is to pay it down with intentionality. You have to lay out a game plan, live on less than you make, and focus with intensity, in order to clean up your debt situation.

Getting Your Snowball on a Roll:

The Most Effective Way to Pay Off Debt!

The method of choice that has been proven to effectively pay off debt, and my professional recommendation, because it has proven to actually work for both my clients and myself, is the "debt snowball" method. The debt snowball obtained its unique name because of how it works to eliminate debt. It literally takes your debts and rolls them into a snowball that grows bigger and bigger as it goes along – like a snowball rolling down a mountain of snow.

Here is how you can create your debt snowball. First, list out all of your debts, from the smallest debt balance to largest debt balance. Second, continue to make all of the minimum monthly payments for all of your debts – except the smallest one. With your prepared monthly budget, figure out exactly how much money you have, that can be allocated towards your debt. Apply that amount to the first debt. Continue applying this money to the first debt until it is paid off.

Once the first debt is paid off, roll all of the money that you were applying to the first debt, into making payments on the second debt (resulting in paying the minimum payment for the second debt plus the money you had been using on the first debt). At this point, your debt snowball is getting bigger! Once you completely pay off the second debt, go through the same process to approach the third debt, adding the total monthly payment that was going towards the second debt to the third debt. Continue this process until your debt snowball is massive and causing destruction to your debt balances like dynamite!

Power Move 2 Example

	Min.	Extra	Total
Card 1	$30	$20	$50
Card 2	$80	$50	$130
Car	$300	$130	$430
Student Loan	$250	$430	$680

To make the debt snowball method of paying off debt a little clearer, consider the following example. Let's say that you have four debts: Credit Card 1, Credit Card 2, Auto Loan, and Student Loans. They are listed in order from the smallest balance to the largest balance. After completing your budget, you find that you have an extra $20 to go towards eliminating your debt, while still continuing to make the minimum payments on all of your other debts each month.

The minimum payment that you must make towards Card 1 each month is $30. When you add the extra $20 to it, you have $50 going towards Card 1 each month. After a few months, Credit Card 1 is completely paid off.

Next, you would take the $50 that you were paying towards Credit Card 1 and use it to make payments on Credit Card 2. The minimum payment for Credit Card 2 each month is $80. Thus, when you add the additional $50 that you had been using on Credit Card 1, to the payment, your payment towards the balance for Credit Card 2 would be $130 each month. After a few months of making the increased payments, Credit Card 2 is paid off.

Next, you would take the $130 that you were paying on Credit Card 2 and apply it to your Auto Loan payment. The monthly payment you are required to make for your Auto Loan is $300. When you add the $130 to it, the total that you would pay towards your Auto Loan balance each month is $430. After making this payment for some time, you completely pay off your car. I assure you that it will ride a lot better when you're not dragging a ball and chain of debt behind you every time you get behind the wheel! Can you see how your snowball is growing?

Now that your Auto Loan is paid off, the last debt remaining is your Student Loans. Your monthly Student Loan payment is $250. When you take the $430 that you had been paying towards your Auto Loan and combine it with your $250 monthly Student Loan payment, you will be paying a whopping $680 each month towards your Student Loan! How amazing is that?

Initially, your snowball started out small, but over time, just like a snowball rolling down the side a mountain of snow, it got bigger and bigger, picking up speed and causing much faster progress in your debt elimination. That is the power and effectiveness of the debt snowball! In fact, it was the debt snowball, plus the temporary increase in income that got me completely out of debt in only 11 months, so I know first-hand that it works effectively. By using this tool, you, too, will be debt free in no time, resulting in your being in a prime position to build wealth!

Additional Coaching Points to Consider as You Pay Off Your Debts...

– Coach's Note 1 –

Celebrate Your Small Wins!

You are engaged in a difficult and challenging process. It is for this reason that when you set and accomplish a milestone of paying off each debt, I encourage you to go out and treat yourself! Celebrating milestones is a great way to keep yourself motivated and excited about the progress you are making. For example, after eliminating the first couple of debts, perhaps you can go out for ice cream or a movie. When you eliminate your last and greatest debt, perhaps you can do something on a grander scale, like plan a weekend trip to California! Whatever you do to celebrate, make sure that it is to scale with what your budget can allow at the time. When you work hard on something like this, you deserve to have a little fun; just make sure that you don't go overboard!

– Coach's Note 2 –

Settle Debts in Collections... for Integrity's Sake

If you have debts that are in collections and that are still outstanding, it is recommended that, for integrity purposes, you include them on the list of debts that you owe (there is no need to address debts that have already been charged off, only those that are outstanding). You gave your word to pay them back when you acquired the debt, and integrity, which is the quality of being honest and having strong moral principles, will call for you to honor your word by paying them back. When you include collections debt on your debt list, do not call or contact the collection agency to arrange payment until you arrive at this debt on the debt list. Contacting them prior to being ready to work on these debts would be premature; there is no need to wake sleeping giants until you are ready feed them!

Also, depending on the balance and the length of time that the account has been past due, you might be able to settle the debt and pay less than the original amount you owed. Most collection agencies will settle for pennies on the dollar, because they purchased the debt from the original debt holder dirt cheap. For example, if you owed $10,000, the collections agency probably bought your debt for $1,500 and would gladly settle with you if you offered them $3,000. This type of scenario results in a win-win for everyone! Just make sure that you save up the cash first, before you attempt to negotiate a settlement with the collection agency. Most importantly, when you pay, whatever you do, never give the collection agency electronic access to your bank account! Some people will set up automatic drafts for a certain installment payment amount with these guys, and before they know it, their entire bank account is wiped clean! If you send them a check, ensure that you send them a certified check, not a personal one; by allowing them to see your routing and bank account numbers on your personal check, you could also inadvertently be giving them access to your accounts. Unfortunately, many collections agencies cannot be trusted; they break the law all of the time. Thus, you must protect yourself from them. They will wipe your account clean if given the opportunity!

Lastly, when you settle a debt that has been in collections, be sure to obtain a letter from the collections agency or credit company stating that the amount settled for has been paid in full.

– Coach's Note 3 –

First Things First: Provide for Your "Four Walls" before All Else!

Sometimes, when clients come to me, they are in such a shaky financial position that they cannot pay all of their bills. Their first question is, "Where do I begin?" My advice to them, and to you, is that if you cannot manage to pay all of your bills, your top priority should be to provide for the four walls of your household, because these four walls are necessary for your survival. Responsibilities that fall within the "four walls" priority are food, utilities, shelter, and transportation – in this exact order.

You must be able to buy food for you and your family. Then, you must make sure your lights and water are on by paying your utility bills. After that, your shelter needs to be secure, because having a place to call home is critical to future success. Lastly, you must be able to pay for transportation expenses so that you can get around to work and to other important places. These basic expenses should be taken care of before attempting to spend on anything else, because without any of these, life would be rather difficult.

It is only after paying for each of these basic expenses – the ones that maintain what goes on within your four walls – that you should even begin to consider purchasing other necessities like clothing. Always address the first things, or the things of highest priority, first. After your basic necessities are taken care of, you can begin looking at how you can address your debt. The last thing you want to do is to be behind on your mortgage but current on your MasterCard and student loans. Following this route will allow you to survive while you figure out a way to generate more income to address your debt.

Power Move 3:

Take the Urgency Out of Emergency!

So far, you have undertaken some major moves, made some big sacrifices, and undoubtedly made some real progress. You should be applauded! You have been living like no one else now, so that later, you can live like no one else. You have laid out your plans, set them in motion, and achieved your goals. You made a conscious decision to change your family tree forever, leaving behind a legacy of wealth instead of one of debt. Doesn't it feel good? Doesn't it feel like a serious amount of weight has already been lifted off your shoulders? Are you starting to feel empowered yet? If not, give it some time, and you will!

Before You Move Ahead, First Celebrate Being DEBT-FREE!

At this point, because you have worked incredibly hard to reach debt freedom, I highly recommend that you treat yourself by saving for a short vacation, buying yourself a nice gift, or doing a fun activity that you like to do – one that would have cost too much before you became debt-free!

For my debt freedom celebration, I went to Las Vegas with some of my fraternity brothers for the weekend. While in Las Vegas, I did what many car enthusiasts would consider a dream: I raced a Ferrari F430 Scuderia around Las Vegas Motor Speedway. When purchased brand new, this car's starting retail price is about $187,000! There I was, completely debt-free, and pushing my dream exotic car around a track. It was a blast! I can still hear the exhaust note in my head as I floored it, speeding down the straight away. It is a moment that I will never forget!

I share my own debt freedom celebration story to emphasize the importance of celebrating such a monumental milestone. Achieving debt freedom is a big deal in our debt-strapped society. When you finally reach it, I want you to forever remember the moment by attaching it to something memorable!

Prepare Yourself: Emergencies Are On the Way!

Now that you are completely debt-free and have treated yourself for achieving such a wonderful milestone, it's time to get back to completing your financial empowerment process! While it is true that getting out of debt is critical to becoming financially empowered, having a fully-funded emergency fund is also key. Consider your emergency fund in the same light as your insurance: it costs you money to protect your assets and saves you from having to go into debt when emergencies arise.

To not have an emergency fund is to set yourself up to quickly fall right back into debt. In fact, research reports that the typical American is unable to cover a $5,000 emergency without going into debt. This is pretty scary, because emergencies are inevitable! The only way to weather these emergencies and remain debt-free, is to have the money already in hand, waiting on them to arrive. In fact, research predicts that in a 10-year span, more than 70% of us will encounter a major financial emergency. Emergency funds ensure that you are prepared for what is inevitably headed your way!

So many people go through life looking for deep, philosophical lessons, when some of life's best teachers are all around us providing a valuable education for us every day. For instance, consider the weather. Some days the weather is filled with sunshine without a cloud in the sky. Some days it's cloudy. Then there are days when it is raining. These are great lessons about the patterns our finances follow throughout life. There are going to be financially sunny times when everything is just perfect; on these days, you couldn't lose if you tried! There are going to be financially cloudy times when things are so-so. Then, there are going to be financially rainy times when everything that can go wrong will go wrong. This means that we have to be prepared; we must establish a means of personal protection from rainy days. Grandma always did say to "save for a rainy day." I have come to realize that she was a lot wiser than I thought.

Cash for a Rainy Day: Fully Funding Your

Emergency Fund

Right now, you should already have a starter emergency fund; this was a task assigned in Power Move 1. Now, it is time to take your emergency fund to the next level by ensuring that it is fully funded!

A fully-funded emergency fund should consist of three to six months' worth of your regular household expenses. For example, if it costs you $2,000 a month to run your household, your emergency fund should be between $6,000 and $12,000. Each household's emergency fund will be different for two reasons: 1) each household's expenses are different, and 2) it is up to each family to determine how many months' worth of expenses it will save (between three and six).

One of the primary factors to consider when establishing your emergency fund, is your type of employment. If you work for yourself, or if you are in sales, you might not bring home the same amount of income each month. Since your income fluctuates, it might be a better idea to save six months' worth of expenses for your household, because your income is less predictable. On the other hand, if you are a government employee and have been with your agency for a long time, you have had a predictable, consistent income for some time. Perhaps three months' worth of expenses would be appropriate for your household, since you are at a job that is more consistent and that has little turnover, resulting in greater job stability. Regardless of which end of the emergency fund spectrum you choose, as long as you are able to save between three to six months' worth of household expenses, you will be in good shape for any emergency that comes your way.

As you are building your emergency fund, keep in mind that

the monies should not be stored anywhere fancy. A simple checking, savings or money market account is perfect. Yes, I know that these accounts do not generate any kind of return or growth on your money; in this case, that is completely fine. Remember: the purpose of this fund is to protect you from when life happens, so you will want the funds to be immediately and easily accessible – not tied up in some investment account that will require extra time and effort before you can gain access to your money.

Finally, though I know that I should not have to say this, I am compelled to say it anyway: your emergency fund should only be used in the case of a real emergency. In fact, once you build your emergency fund, it is important to not even think about it being there. Forget that it exists! If you are always conscious that your money is just sitting there in the bank, you will find a reason to create an artificial emergency. However, needing to buy a new couch is not an emergency. Needing a new outfit for this weekend's night out on the town is not an emergency. In contrast, your water heater exploding would be a great example of an emergency. If at any time you do have to dip into the emergency fund to address a real emergency, it is important to replenish those funds immediately.

Your emergency fund is important; it is your very own personal debt protection mechanism. It is your first line of defense to protect your financial freedom! Think of it as your personal Ray Lewis (the famous NFL Hall of Fame line-backer) that protects your bank account from being scored in by your opponent – debt! Without an emergency fund in place, it is only a matter of time before you get your financial world rocked; one of these days, it is going to rain, and an emergency is going to occur, so have your defense funds ready!

Looking to Buy a House? Now is the Time!

Since you have completely funded your emergency fund and you are free of debt, if you were looking to buy a house, now is the time, because you are in just the right position to make such a major purchase! You have created the room in your income to do so!

As you begin your house hunt, seek to purchase a home that you can see yourself living in for a very long time; buy your dream home, if you can afford it. Each of us has in mind what we would consider to be our "dream home". For some, a dream home would be a cute, small bungalow in the city, while for others, a dream home would be a large mansion-like home located just outside of the city. Every person's idea of what qualifies as a dream home is different, varying by size, style, cost, and location.

My advice to you is to purchase your dream home at the price point that you can afford. Purchase the home with the mindset that you will own it forever, because you fully intend to pay it off. Of course, if life happens once you've paid the house off and you have to move, at least it was a home that you enjoyed while you were in it. However, since you have paid it off, you now have options: you can keep it and use it as an investment property, or you can sell it and get a nice chunk of change for it that you can use to buy another home.

If you are considering making a home purchase as an investment property, my advice to you is to wait! First, pay off your own home (Power Move 6). Then, after your home is paid off and you are ready to buy an investment property, spare yourself the unnecessary money, time, and stress by buying the new property with cash. I say this because if your renter moves out or stops paying, the last thing that you want is to end up with your finances in shambles because you now have to pay for an additional mortgage. So many people purchase investment properties – multiplying them like rabbits – in an attempt to build wealth rapidly, but because they make these purchases prematurely (before they have executed the necessary preceding Power Moves), such purchases hurt them rather than help them build wealth.

Remember: no matter how many times you read the story The Tortoise and the Hare, the tortoise wins every time! Slow and steady wins the race. Pay off your own home first, and then, only after your own home is secured, purchase your investment property with cash money. Trust me: you will appreciate this route much better, because it will actually help you win the race!

Getting a Mortgage Is Acceptable IF You Can

Follow the Rules!

In order to maintain your state of financial freedom, the preferred method of purchasing a home should be cash. Before you dismiss this is as an option, know that it is indeed possible and has been accomplished by many! However, it is understood that the great majority of people will not be able to wait so long to purchase a home. Thus, if you do have to take out a mortgage to finance the purchasing of a home, please follow these three guidelines that are designed to keep you financially empowered during and after the home buying process!

Mortgage Guideline 1:   Save Up at Least a 20% Down Payment

Before you buy a home, you should save up at least 20% of the appraised value or sale price of the house as a down payment. Putting 20% down on the purchase of the house will help you to avoid having to pay private mortgage insurance, more commonly known as "PMI". PMI protects your lender in case you default on your loan payments. With this insurance, you, the borrower, pay the premiums. If the insurance ever needed to be paid out because you defaulted on your loan payments, your lender would be the beneficiary of the insurance pay-out. PMI fees vary, depending on the size of the down payment and the loan amount, usually varying from around 0.3 percent to 1.15 percent of the original loan amount per year.

For example, let's say that you are buying a $200,000 house and make a 10 percent down payment. Your 10 percent down payment would equate to $20,000, meaning that you are borrowing $180,000. The PMI mortgage insurer charges an annual premium of 0.75 percent. Thus, the insurer multiplies the loan amount by 0.0075, for an annual premium of $1,350. Divided into 12 monthly payments, this is $112.50, which you must pay every month with your mortgage. Depending on the amount borrowed, this could equate to you spending hundreds or even thousands of dollars a year! There is no need to spend extra money when you don't have to, so save up your 20% down payment, and avoid the PMI expense altogether.

Mortgage Guideline 2: Use a 15-Year Mortgage

If you must borrow money from a mortgage lender to purchase your home, please use a 15-year mortgage (big emphasis on the please)! If you finance your home for anything more than a 15-year mortgage, you will easily pay double, if not triple, the cost of the value of your home. Many people get into 30-year mortgages because the payments are cheaper than those of a 15-year mortgage; they plan to double their monthly payments and still pay off the home in 15 years. However, the sad reality is that most people are unable to stick to this plan. What was supposed to be an extra house payment ends up being spent on other things. As a result, they end up paying for their home two to three times over, because their payments, including interest and other fees, are spread over 30 years.

To illustrate the benefits of securing a 15-year mortgage as opposed to a 30-year mortgage, let's continue with the previous example. If you were to take out a 15-year mortgage for $180,000 at a 5 percent interest rate with a PMI of .75 percent, your monthly payment would be $1,631.76. Your total payments over the life of the loan would sum up to be $293,717.14. Now, let's say that you took out a 30-year mortgage according to the same terms. For a 30-year mortgage, your monthly payment would be $1,174.61. Your total payments over the life of the loan would sum up to be $422,860.41.

As you can see, the monthly payment for the 30-year mortgage is almost $500 cheaper than the 15-year mortgage; this is why most people go the 30-year mortgage route. Sadly, such a route will result, in this case, in you paying two and a half times the loan balance you originally took out. Just imagine what that money could do for you or your family! Thus, be financially wise, and go the 15-year mortgage route.

Mortgage Guideline 3:   Keep Your Monthly Payments Below 25 Percent

If you will take out a mortgage, keep in mind as you are house-hunting and considering how much house you can afford, that your house payment should be no more than 25 percent of your take-home pay. In order to financially prosper, it is imperative that you keep your house payment below 25 percent for two reasons. The first reason is the more obvious one: you don't want your house payment taking up too much of your income, because you want to have the flexibility to be able to do other things with your income, such as invest for retirement and for your kids' college funds (Power Moves 4 and 5), while living comfortably. There are a lot of people whose retirements are underfunded, and saving for their kids' college funds is not even a possibility because they have too much house! Having too much house can also put you in the position to have to take on debt, which results in more cash leaving your account each month. For example, since your house has taken up so much of your money, you do not have the cash flow to save for a car; thus, you might need to finance the purchase of a car by signing up for a car payment. Having to make these payments each month further restricts your income!

The second reason that you should keep your house payment below 25 percent, is that you do not want your income tied up; when life happens, you don't want your world rocked because you don't have access to any money. In 2008, many people lost their homes due to tough economic conditions, which resulted in pay cuts and job losses for millions of Americans. When combined with the burst of the real estate bubble, this led to literally millions of foreclosures around the nation. However, this is no surprise; people were living in homes with monthly payments that were, in some cases, more than 50 percent of their take-home pay!

If you make the mistake of allowing your monthly house payment to be too high, if something were to happen – like a pay cut or a job loss – and you also did not have a completely funded emergency fund, you would instantly find yourself in an unpleasant situation. I firmly believe in learning from the mistakes of others. Do not allow what has happened to millions of other Americans, happen to you; keep your house payments within a range that you can reasonably afford – 25 percent or below. Yes, this might mean that you have to get a smaller house, but at least your house will be in line with your budget! Then, later on, when your household income increases, or you pay your home off (Power Move 6), you can always upgrade to a larger home!

Power Move 4:

Invest Today for a Comfortable Tomorrow!

Congratulations! You've made a lot of progress so far on your financial journey! Up to this point, you are debt-free, and you have a fully-funded emergency fund, and for this, I applaud you! Now, it is time to take your financial empowerment to the next level – through investing!

In Power Move 1, you will recall that I asked you to temporarily stop investing so that you could harness the power of your income as you declared war on your debt. Since your debt has been eliminated, you are now in full control of your most powerful wealth building tool: your income! At this point, you are in a much better position to build wealth, because you are financially empowered, and you – not your creditors or life's little emergencies – can dictate where your income goes. Now, it is time to hit the "Play" button and resume investing, so that you can take your level of financial empowerment to new heights. With all of the progress you have made, you can now afford to invest a solid amount of money while still being able to live comfortably. That's quite a power position!

You Won't Stay Young Forever, So Build Your "Nest Egg" Now!

If you possess any level of foresight and wisdom, you know that each day you are getting older, and eventually your body will not be able to do what it is doing today. One day you will not have the capacity, and let's face it, the desire, to work anymore. Considering this, it is important to start saving for the day that we can no longer work for our money – the day we must depend on our money working for us.

Many of us have sadly witnessed the financial stresses of our parents being broke, not being able to retire, and even having to sign up for reverse mortgages in order to financially survive. Unfortunately, this is too common a phenomenon in our society. The even sadder reality is that our society is no longer outraged when people work hard for decades, only to get to the end and have nothing left – no source of sustainability. The truth is that they – and we – should all know better. We live in an era that is filled with information on how to save, invest, and retire comfortably. However, despite the abundance of resources that exist to show us how to do so, millions of young people continue to follow in the footsteps of their broke parents every day. It's time to break the cycle.

It is obvious that in the later years of our lives, we will not be able to work and generate income with the same amount of energy that was available to us in our younger years. We aren't young forever. In light of this, we need to have a plan that will enable us to build enough of a "nest egg" to be able to live comfortably in the later years of our lives. If not, our only alternatives will be to either be broke and/or to be a burden to our children. Neither of these is any way to live. Thus, why not build a legacy instead of destroying yours, bringing it to a tragic – and broke – end? Make the resolve to live differently tomorrow by investing today!

How Much, When, and Where? The Ins and Outs of Investing!

When you begin investing, it is recommended that you invest 15 percent of your gross income (gross income is your income before taxes). For example, if someone makes a gross income of $50,000 a year, 15 percent of this would be $7,500 annually, or $625 per month. You might wonder, "Why 15 percent of my income?" As a rule of thumb, 15 percent is a good percentage of your income to invest because it allows you to build your retirement nest egg at a steady rate, while still allowing you to live a comfortable life, because it does not tie up too much of your income.

The fact that you are now debt-free and have eliminated all of your consumer debt, means that you should be able to invest 15 percent without even noticing; this is exactly the reason that we approach financial empowerment in this particular order. To try to pay off debt while simultaneously trying to invest would be quite ineffective; most people would not be able to invest anywhere near 15 percent under such circumstances. In fact, one of the reasons why many people reach retirement without enough money saved, is because they simply did things out of order! Remember: the power of focusing on the right things at the right times, determines how much we get done and how effectively.

Now that you know how much to invest, you might

wonder when you should invest. The answer to this question is easy: yesterday! However, if you have not already started consistently investing, there is an alternative answer: now! In order to achieve maximum return on your investment, it is critical that you start investing as early as possible. In doing so, you can establish a comfortable means of retirement while at the same time changing your family tree by injecting wealth into it!

Here is a prime and practical example of how investing 15 percent of your gross income can change your family tree. Meet Marcus and Jackie, a married couple, both 25 years old. Together, they make a combined gross income of $48,000 a year. At age 25, they began investing 15 percent of their gross income, which was $600 a month, and they continued investing until they both reached the age of 65. If invested at the Dow Jones Industrial average of 9 percent over the last 30 years, by the age of 65, they would have approximately $2,531,543.44! Do you see how critical it is to start investing early?

Take note that this example operated under the assumption that neither Marcus nor Jackie ever got an increase in income. It was also assumed that they never invested more than 15 percent of the income with which they started. However, for either assumption to be supported in a real-life scenario is highly unlikely, since most people's careers and salaries increase over time; in light of this, they are able to invest more. Even if my math was halfway wrong, Marcus and Jackie would still have $1.2 million more than they would have had!

If you govern your financial life according to the principles of the seven Power Moves, there is no way that you should retire broke. We must be willing to sacrifice our current comforts of today in order to live a comfortable tomorrow during our retirement years! Fifteen percent of our gross income is a small price to pay for a financially secure future, so get out of debt and free up your income so that you can begin – sooner than later – building wealth like never before!

The next area of focus is where you should invest. Ideally, you should invest in pre-tax plans such as your company's 401k/403b and Traditional or ROTH IRA's (Individual Retirement Account). These accounts are specifically designated for retirement, and as a result, they come with tax benefits. In fact, section 401k and section 403b are the actual sections within the tax code where you can find information on these investment accounts.

The difference between a 401k and a 403b is that a 401k is used by for-profit companies, and a 403b is used by non-profit 501(c)(3) organizations like public education systems, hospitals, and self-employed ministers. Most organizations offer employees some type of match, meaning that whatever monthly contribution the employee invests into the retirement account, the employer will "match" the contribution by also contributing the exact same amount. However, an employer often has a limit of how much it will match in contributions to your retirement account.

If your employer offers a match, take full advantage of the match by contributing as much to the plan as the employer will match. Keep in mind that the match percentage contributed by your employer should not be considered as a part of the 15 percent that you are personally investing for retirement. Instead, consider your employer's matched contribution extra gravy on top. Therefore, if your company matches 5 percent of your contribution, you should invest 5 percent of your 15 percent with your company, and then you should invest the remaining 10 percent into your own IRA account.

The ROTH IRA vs. the Traditional IRA: Which Is Best for Me?

As you prepare to open an individual retirement account, or IRA, you should be aware of the rules governing each type, so that you can make the best choice for your situation. Ultimately, the main difference between each of the various types of retirement accounts is the tax treatment.

The first type of IRA is the Traditional IRA. Anyone can open a Traditional IRA. Once opened, if you are under the age of 50, you are allowed to contribute up to $5,500 per year into your IRA (under current tax law). If you are 50 years old or older, you are allowed to contribute up to $6,500 per year into your IRA (under current tax law). With a Traditional IRA, you make contributions to your account before taxes; this results in less of your income being taxed by the government right now. However, upon retirement, withdrawals will be taxed at a percentage that is based on your income bracket at that time.

The second type of IRA is the Roth IRA. With a Roth IRA, you make contributions to your account after taxes; this results in less money being placed into your account. The great thing about this, however, is that your money is allowed to grow tax free and will not be taxed when you withdraw funds at retirement.

While both plans have their pros and cons, I personally prefer the Roth IRA option. Most people will make the most of their money at the later stages of their lives, because over time, they will advance in their careers, move up the corporate ladder, or experience expansion in their businesses. Considering this, you are more than likely in the lowest tax bracket that you will ever occupy, right now. Therefore, why not lock in your tax rate today by paying taxes on the retirement funds you deposit into your IRA right now? Plus you never know what future tax rates are going to be since tax laws frequently change.

On the contrary, it could be said that someone might plan to occupy a lower tax bracket during retirement than he occupies now, because he will live on less money after he retires. Thus, it might be better to make pre-tax contributions into a Traditional IRA and wait to pay taxes until later on after retirement when the taxes will be less. This is a strong consideration. If you do not plan to supplement your retirement income by running a business or doing anything else to generate any additional income during your retirement years, the Traditional IRA approach might be better for you. Ultimately, the choice is up to you and what you prefer.

Stocks vs. Mutual Funds:

Which Investment Option Should I Choose?

Depending on with whom you open your retirement account, you will be provided with the option of investing in either stocks or mutual funds, or both. Prior to making this decision, it is important to be informed about the workings of each option, so that you can choose the type of investment that will work best for both your lifestyle and your financial progress.

Stocks are individual shares of ownership of a particular company that can be purchased by an investor; when you invest in a company's stock, you actually own a small percentage of the company. If the company has great value, even your small percentage of ownership can also carry great value. However, if the company begins to lose value, so does your stock, and consequently, so does your investment account.

In my opinion, stocks are too risky an investment option for the average person today, because being a successful investor in the stock market requires spending time tracking and monitoring the stock market's daily performance. When companies seem to be on the rise or promising to yield high profits in the near future, investors will buy stock in them, for they stand to make money. When companies seem to be faltering and losing money, or if it is forecasted that they will see low or no profit, investors will sell, because they stand to lose money. Thus, when you invest in stock, you have to pay close attention to the daily fluctuations of the market, because all of your wealth is riding on the stocks of the few companies that you have invested in.

Having stock in a "few companies" is in and of itself is problematic; most people tend to only invest in a choice few stocks, because they do not know how to appropriately balance a stock portfolio. A balanced stock portfolio is one that is diversified. It is comprised of a variety of industries such that the strengths of one industry's earnings can compensate for the weaknesses of another industry's earnings. When all, or the great majority, of your stock is tied into one industry, when that industry takes a nosedive, so does the great majority of your wealth! The bottom line is that if you do not have time to carefully watch the stock market and focus on deliberately managing your stock portfolio, investing in stocks might not be the best option for you.

Mutual funds, on the other hand, are a great investment for the typical person who just wants to work 30 to 40 years, invest money into his retirement account without having to keep a close eye on it, and then retire and live off his returns. There are several different types of mutual funds: International, Income, Growth, and Growth & Income mutual funds. I recommend each of these in order to have a diverse and balanced portfolio. International mutual funds take advantage of the international market. Income mutual funds invest in companies like Walmart, which always earn income regardless of whether the financial climate is good or bad. Growth mutual funds invest in growing companies like the new and rapidly growing transportation company Uber, which is taking the luxury rental car service market by storm. Growth & Income mutual funds invest in companies like Google, who earn a lot of income while at the same time are growing and expanding in new directions. The presence of each of these types of funds will ensure that your investment portfolio has the balance and diversity it needs to weather the ups and downs of the market.

Mutual funds are a much easier and more manageable investment option for people who just want to invest their money and watch it grow without having to check on it and deal with it day to day. Another great benefit of mutual funds is that they are automatically diversified and offer investors a wide variety of options; they generally hold a large number of stocks, with each one comprising only a small percentage of the portfolio. Best of all, mutual funds are managed by mutual fund managers whose job is to keep an eye on the performance of the stocks in the fund, in order to produce the highest yield for you! Thus, I consider this the best investment option for the vast majority of people.

To sum up, my advice to you is to keep your investing simple and to diversify. Though we tend to make things much more complicated for ourselves than they have to be, investing does not have to be one of those things! Stuart Wilde, late financial author and speaker, once said, "Money is like manure: left in one pile, it stinks. Spread it around, and it makes things grow." In light of this, I encourage you to heed this advice. Spread your money around, and watch the growth that results!

Power Move 5:
Eliminate the Fees from Your Kids' Degree!

According to the Wall Street Journal, at the time of the writing of this book, 70 percent of students graduating from college had student loan debt, and the average student loan balance was $33,000. Student loans are, by far, the most oppressive form of debt that exists among today's generation. While we applaud the fact that we have more college graduates than ever before in the United States, at what cost have we achieved such a milestone?

Today's Graduates: Hot Air Balloons with a Basket Full of Bricks!

I describe college graduates who graduate with student loan debt as "hot air balloons with a basket full of bricks". Why? Because while the balloon is on the rise, filled with so much potential and so many possibilities, the bricks weigh it down and stifle its progress! For college graduates, the sky is the limit; there is nowhere they cannot go, and there is nothing they cannot do, because their potential for progress is unlimited! However, most of them cannot get off the ground because of the immense weight of student loan debt that holds them down.

If only someone would carefully explain to both parents and students, the tremendous impact that loading college students down with debts that they will have to pay back upon graduation, will have on them in the future. Most people think that student loans are a given for any college student; borrow the money now to get the degree, and then use the degree to help generate the funds to pay back the money later. However, they fail to realize that student loan debt is still debt, and with debt comes the sacrifice of some of your freedoms.

In the case of college students with student loans, taking on these often massive debt loads means the sacrifice of their future freedoms. Though they might be able to secure a good job, they cannot easily take a sabbatical from work. Though their heart and life's passion might be to be with a company that pays less, they have to compromise and work for the company that pays more, in order to make their monthly loan payments. Though they desire to travel and see the world, they cannot do so, because they have no discretionary income. Though they have always dreamt of starting a business, this dream is indefinitely postponed, because they simply cannot afford to; they must keep working, because they have loan payments to make.

These are not the only sacrifices that tens of millions of students and graduates who carry debt from student loans are forced to make; the effects of this form of debt are far reaching. Student loan debt is also causing delays in home buying, marriage, and purchases of better vehicles, particularly among younger generations. Rachel Cruze, a New York Times best-selling author and daughter of financial guru Dave Ramsey, writes, "Student loans are the roadblock of this generation of students." We can clearly see why she made such a statement. We should also clearly see that we must work to forge a better path for our own children who will attend college in the future.

Setting Our Kids Up for Future Success: What's Your College Plan?

In Power Move 2, we addressed paying off your student loan debt. Now, it is time to be proactive in helping your children win in college; Power Move 5 is to simply establish college funding for them! It is only by accumulating the resources that our children need to pay for college before they get to college that we will be able to stop the trend of young people taking on massive debt loads before they even step into the real world and start living! Let's not cripple our children by offering them debt as a solution to pay for college; instead, let's empower them by giving them the chance to win financially.

To win with college funding, it is imperative that you begin planning and investing for college expenses when your child is born. Many parents wait until their children become teenagers before they start trying to figure out how they will pay for their college tuition, and by then, it is way too late. One of the most popular solutions that parents tend to turn to in order to fund their children's college accounts or to pay for college is that of pausing their own retirement savings process and redirecting the monies towards their children's college funding. As noble as this seems, however, this is a huge mistake! What starts as skipping a few contributions to the 401(k) often ends with raiding the balance to put a child through college. This compromises the parents' financial future as well as the financial stability of the entire family!

If you already have children, especially older children, and have not yet begun to plan for how you will pay for their college expenses, it is officially time to play catch up! You will need to act with a greater sense of urgency during Power Move 5, for example, than someone whose children have not yet started attending primary school.

The 529 Plan or the Education Saving Account:

Which is the Best Education Investment Account for My Family?

When investing for college, I recommend the use of a special education investment account. You could invest in things like savings bonds, but I consider this to be one of the worst investments to save for college, because you do not get any real growth or ROI (return on investment). All you really have is the money that you have put into the bond. While you could also use other options such as mutual funds or stock to invest for your child's future education, these investments do not carry the tax benefits associated with education investment accounts. The most popular education investment accounts are state 529 Plans and Education Savings Accounts (ESA), both of which can be used simultaneously.

A 529 Plan is an education savings plan that is operated by a state or educational institution. Designed to encourage parents to save for the costs of college in the future, this plan allows you to contribute a certain amount of after-tax money into your account before your child turns 18 years old. The money that you contribute into the account grows tax-free, and it is not subject to federal or state taxation when it is spent on qualified education expenses, such as tuition, fees, books, and room and board. Just about every state in the U.S. has its own 529 Plan. Parents, regardless of which state they live in or in which state their children will attend college, have the liberty of investing in any state's 529 Plan that they choose. Each state's respective 529 Plan offers different benefits and features, so before selecting a plan, be sure to do your research to find the one that works best for your family!

An Education Savings Account, or ESA, is a federal account that is created for the sole purpose of paying for a qualified education, much like a 529 Plan. However, in contrast to a 529 Plan which typically allows contributions in excess of $300,000, contributions to an ESA are limited to $2,000 per year until the child turns 18 years old. Also, unlike contributions to a 529 Plan, which are allowed to stay in the Plan's account indefinitely (and can even be used for retirement purposes, subject to penalties and fees), the account balance for an ESA must be completely utilized by the time the child or beneficiary turns 30 years old (age requirements and restrictions are waived for an ESA if the beneficiary has special needs). One big difference between the 529 Plan and the ESA, however, is a unique advantage that only the ESA offers: it can also be used to pay for private school during your child's grade school years. Personally, I prefer the 529 Plans, because they provide more flexibility and more options for investment, and because they are state sponsored, so greater levels of confidence can be placed in them. I also prefer them because you can put a lot more into a 529 Plan than you can into an ESA.

It pays to start investing in your child's educational invest-ment account early! If a couple was to invest $150 per month from the time their child was born until the time the child reached 18 years old, at a rate of 9%, once the child turned 18 and was ready to off to college, they would have approximately $77,361! This is a considerable start to funding a child's college education, es-pecially considering how easily we can blow through spend-ing $150 in a month. This would be equivalent to what some people spend on their sophisticated coffee drinks or a cable bill!

All said, there is no excuse for not finding a way to invest at least $150 a month towards your child's financial future. With college planning as well as other types of investing and financial money management, you should see a recurring theme: start early! Only by starting early – starting now – will you be able to achieve maximum gains without having to make excessive modifications to your finances and lifestyle.

Power Move 6:

Make Your House a Home, Not a Prison, by Paying It Off!

If you were to ask a few typical people what their dreams for the future consisted of, you would inevitably hear owning their own home as part of that dream (which usually also includes a successful career and a happy family). This is understandable! Having a homestead, a place that we can call our very own, or a home base, represents comfort, stability, safety, security, family, and love. In fact, it is often said that "home is where the heart is". Our homes represent us – our geography, our identity, and our lifestyle – and they mean the world to us. It is for this reason that it is so critical that we secure this vital aspect of our financial future as soon as we possibly can!

Being "House Poor" and Imprisoned by

Mortgage Debt

Is No Way to Live!

Unfortunately, once many people take the big step of purchasing a home, this aspect of their dream for a beautiful future becomes a nightmare! Oftentimes, these are the people who buy too much house, purchasing a more expensive home than their budgets can afford. In addition to being constantly strapped for cash, in some cases their financial conditions become so restricted that they miss mortgage payments and are faced with foreclosure.

These are people that are referred to as being "house poor", and it is a sad reality that this describes millions of American homeowners today. People who are house poor purchased too much house, and as a result, they are struggling financially and cannot get ahead in life; their mortgage payments are leaving no room for them to build wealth with their income. This is no way to live! To avoid becoming house poor, heed the advice offered in Power Move 3: keep your mortgage payment at 25 percent or less of your take-home pay.

Another way that home ownership tends to threaten our efforts to build wealth is through people's decisions to borrow money with 30-year mortgages, which they pay for the full 30 years, allowing their debt to hang around forever. In such cases, they have turned home ownership into a prison sentence in which they are condemned to live in debt for decades, versus being free to use their income to help them build wealth.

While home ownership represents many things for the psyche, I also firmly believe that owning a home outright represents one of the quickest and most necessary ways to build wealth. When you set out to purchase a home, your main focus should be to eventually own it outright, eliminating all payments from your life. How is this accomplished? By paying off your mortgage in far less time than the terms of your mortgage stipulate, so that you can free up your income and set yourself on the path to truly build wealth. Thus, in Power Move

6 you want to focus on paying off your home as quickly as possible!

Pay Off Your House as Quickly as Possible!

By this point in your financial empowerment journey, your retirement plan is set up, intact, and being funded consistently and your children's college funding is underway. Now, it's time to revisit your budget while asking yourself, "Is there any discretionary income available?" Any discretionary income that you have at this point should now be used to attack the principal balance on your house. For example, after doing your monthly budget and covering all of your usual monthly expenses, retirement contributions, and kids' college investments, you might have some extra income left over. You should take this extra income and apply it to your mortgage payment. Paying on your home – and eventually paying it off – puts you in the best possible position to build wealth. Imagine how much money you could accumulate if you didn't have a house payment! Imagine how quickly you could afford vacations or buy a new car by freeing up this income!

As you approach paying off your house during this Power Move, do not look at your home as simply an investment; look at it more as a way to increase your net worth by no longer throwing money away on rent or mortgage payments. When you finally do own your home outright, you will not only realize a higher net worth and financial power like never before, but you will build upon the legacy that you are seeking to establish through your financial empowerment journey. Why? Because rather than starting with nothing and ending with nothing as generation after generation seems to do, you might have started at the bottom, but your legacy will end with great wealth! Not only do you have the privilege of saying that you are debt-free, but you have cash in your accounts, assets through your investments, and best of all, you have a home that is completely owned outright! In putting yourself in such a position, you are leaving a legacy that will live well beyond the time that you leave the earth, and you will change your family tree forever!

Power Move 7:

More Money = More Options to Give & Live!

Welcome to Power Move 7 – the final Power Move! Undoubtedly, as you have carefully navigated this financial empowerment journey, your life has changed for the better in many regards. You are now in control of your money; you live according to a plan; your life of debt is long gone; payments are no more; and financial freedom is a reality! What a beautiful position to be in!

I firmly believe that this is the kind of life that each of us was created to live – a life free of financial stress, which is known to lead to other life problems. We should be able to live our lives in such a way that we can focus on the things that are most important to us, like our loved ones, our ambitions, our dreams, and our passions! However, while everyone desires to live like this, you have actually done the work to position yourself to actually do it! You are now at a place that most other people will only ever dream of achieving: you have options on how you will live. For this, I offer to you a hearty "Congratulations!"

Re-evaluations, Making Donations, and FUN!

The Final Few Steps of the Journey

This final Power Move that you will make begins with first re-evaluating your retirement goals. Are you on target to live the kind of life that you desire to live when you retire? Use a retirement calculator (a basic one can be found online) to determine whether you are going to be able to meet your lifestyle goa,l based upon your current level of contributions to your retirement fund. If not, you might find that now is the time to increase your contributions. The best part is that increasing your contributions should not be a problem, because now, you have no house payment! How awesome is that?

Next, I encourage you to start giving charitable donations to those in need around you. Give to your place of worship, a local shelter, a family member in need, the homeless guy on the corner or to whomever you can lend a helping hand. One might ask, "Why give?" The answer is clear: we are all managers of the resources that our Creator has put in our possession. Therefore, we are asked to give some, save some, and spend some – in that exact order.

Giving not only benefits the receiver; more importantly, it benefits the giver. How so? Giving makes people less selfish and births higher levels of compassion for others. Less-selfish people also have a tendency to prosper in relationships; in case you didn't know, relationships are the most important things in life. Then, people with great relationships tend to be happier and more positive than people who do not have great relationships, whether these relationships are family relationships, business relationships, or just friendships.

What's more, those who have wonderful relationships tend to have more opportunities passed their way; people tend to help and do business with positive people whom they trust. These opportunities, in turn, lead to more wealth creation.

Therefore, as you can see, being a giver has its benefits; it makes a tremendous impact on who an individual is or becomes, so let's give, to empower our communities and to empower ourselves!

Lastly, it's time that you enjoyed that money! You've earned it! You've lived like no one else, so now you can live like no one else. You were willing to make whatever sacrifices you made to get to where you are – now is the time to do your victory dance! You've shown maturity by delaying pleasure of the here and now for the greater good – and a greater future, which you are now in!

Now, it's time to do the things that you have always wanted to do like travel the world, buy investment property, purchase a brand new car, pay off your parents' mortgage, or whatever it is that you always desired in your heart to do. What's amazing is that you can cash-flow all of these things for the rest of your life, simply because you made a decision to change your family tree forever. What a way to live! Now, you are living the life you were always intended to live, because you are now in a position to have the freedom to do so! Congratulations – now live the dream!

Bonus Chapter:

Common Personal Finance Myths – EXPOSED!

MYTH 1:

Credit card reward points are free, so you might as well take advantage of them!

Wrong! In case you haven't heard, nothing in life is free – including reward points! Credit card companies are in business to make money. Giving away free cash and reward points takes money out of their pockets. Considering this, do you really think that these freebies are actually free? The truth is that credit card companies invest millions of dollars into research that is designed to figure out how to get you to spend money using their cards. Why? Because they make money every time you swipe your card!

The merchant or retailer selling your purchased items pays a percentage fee to the credit card company, which covers the cost of the reward points. However, what the credit card companies really rely on is that by using your credit card frequently (to rack up those "free" points), the chances of you not paying the card balance off every month increases. As a matter of fact, about 40 percent of Americans will not pay off their credit card balances at the end of the month; not only do credit card companies know this – they bank on it! As a result of not paying off your balances, credit card companies can charge you interest fees (often as high as 25 percent!) on the balance that you carry, which means that they make money!

Reward points and cash back programs are great marketing ploys to get you to constantly keep using your credit card; they want you to pursue these points so that they can make more money. However, as I said, these companies are in business to make money, not lose it.

MYTH 2:

Credit cards are safe!

Sorry to bust your bubble, but this myth is also false! Credit card companies want you to believe that credit cards are completely safe so that you can get one of their credit cards and use it frequently! Just in case you haven't gotten the hint yet, I will say it again: your use of their credit cards is how they get paid!

The safer option is to use a debit card. I refer to them as "safe", because if your cards are used fraudulently by someone else, you can call the card company, report the use, and not be liable for the charges. In this way, debit card transactions can be just as safe as using credit cards, because the transactions are protected by the card processing company (like Visa or MasterCard) when you run them as credit cards. When you run a debit card as a debit purchase, you will be required to enter your PIN (Personal Identification Number). Entering your PIN number makes the use of your debit card less secure, because in today's high-tech world, PIN theft is very easy.

To have your debit card transactions secured, as you are making your purchase, simply run your debit card as credit. Doing so will eliminate the need for you to enter your PIN, though the retailer will ask you for signature on a receipt (gas stations will require you to enter your zip code instead of signing a receipt).

MYTH 3:

You should have a mortgage so that you can write off the interest paid on your taxes!

This myth is false – though one of the most widely perpetuated myths I have heard! People who subscribe to this myth believe that paying off their home is not the way to go, because if they do so, they will not be able to get the annual write-off of their mortgage interest on their taxes. Let me get this right: so, you want to send thousands of dollars to the bank, just to be able to write off the interest portion of your mortgage? What if you had no mortgage payments and instead just paid the taxes? My, how much more money you would have!

Consider this example: Your mortgage is $200,000, financed over 15 years at 4.5 percent. Your monthly payment is $1,530. That means, in your first year, you pay $18,360. Of this amount, your interest is $3,349. According to the myth – and most people's logic – the best route is to pay the mortgage company the $18,360 in order to save $3,349 in taxes. However, why not pay off your home early? In doing so, you will not have to pay the mortgage company anything, and during tax time, if you have to pay, you just pay the taxes of $3,349? Your bank account will thank you when it is $15,011 richer every year as a result of paying off your mortgage. The myth of needing to hold on to your mortgage is just that – a myth. It is so false that a lie detector could detect it!"

BONUS CONTENT

DON'T FORGET TO DOWNLOAD YOUR

Budget Form

At

HTTP://WWW.TRUEFINANCIALCOACHES.COM

FROMPAYCHECKSTOPOWER.COM

FACEBOOK: TRUE FINANCIAL

TWITTER: @SHANNAANDAWDA

INSTAGRAM: @SHANNAANDAWDA

PERISCOPE: SHANNAAN DAWDA

SNAPCHAT: SHANNAANDAWDA

Monthly Cash Flow Plan

Cash flows in and out each month. Make sure you tell it where to go!

TRUE FINANCIAL

Yes, this budget form has a lot of lines and blanks.

But that's okay. We do that so we can list practically every expense imaginable on this form to prevent you from forgetting something. Don't expect to put something on every line. Just use the ones that are relevant to your specific situation.

Step 1

Enter your monthly take-home pay in the box at the top right (**A**). This is the amount you have for the month to budget. So far so good, huh?

A   Monthly Take-Home Pay [   ]

Step 2

Within each main category, such as Food, there are subcategories, like Groceries. Start at the top and work your way down, filling out the Budgeted column (**B**) first. Add up each subcategory and put that number in the Total box (**C**).

Also, pay attention to Dave's recommended percentages (**D**). This will help you keep from budgeting too much for a category.

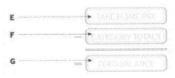

Step 3

Finally, enter your take-home pay in the top box at the end of the page (**E**), then add up all categories and place that total in the Category Totals box (**F**). Then subtract your Category Totals amount from your Take-Home Pay. You should have a zero balance (**G**). Doesn't that feel great?

E   TAKE-HOME PAY
F   CATEGORY TOTALS
G   =   ZERO BALANCE

Step 4

When the month ends, put what you actually spent in the Spent column (**H**). That will help you make any necessary adjustments to the next month's budget.

Monthly Cash Flow Plan

Cash flows in and out each month. Make sure you tell it where to go!

TRUE FINANCIAL

Monthly Take-Home Pay	

Add up budgeted column & enter here

These icons represent good options for cash envelopes

♥ CHARITY	Spent	Budgeted
Tithes		
Charity & Offerings		
*10-15% TOTAL		

🍴 FOOD	Spent	Budgeted
Groceries		
Restaurants		
*5-15% TOTAL		

💰 SAVING	Spent	Budgeted
Emergency Fund		
Retirement Fund		
College Fund		
*10-15% TOTAL		

👕 CLOTHING	Spent	Budgeted
Adults		
Children		
Cleaning/Laundry		
*2-7% TOTAL		

🏠 HOUSING	Spent	Budgeted
First Mortgage/Rent		
Second Mortgage		
Real Estate Taxes		
Repairs/Maint.		
Association Dues		
*25-35% TOTAL		

🚗 TRANSPORTATION	Spent	Budgeted
Gas & Oil		
Repairs & Tires		
License & Taxes		
Car Replacement		
Other		
*10-15% TOTAL		

⚙ UTILITIES	Spent	Budgeted
Electricity		
Gas		
Water		
Trash		
Phone/Mobile		
Internet		
Cable		
*5-10% TOTAL		

🏥 MEDICAL/HEALTH	Spent	Budgeted
Medications		
Doctor Bills		
Dentist		
Optometrist		
Vitamins		
Other		
Other		
*5-10% TOTAL		

*Dave's Recommended Percentages

TRUE FINANCIAL

🛡 INSURANCE

	Spent	Budgeted
Life Insurance		
Health Insurance		
Homeowner/Renter		
Auto Insurance		
Disability Insurance		
Identity Theft		
Long-Term Care		
*10-25% TOTAL		

👤 PERSONAL

	Spent	Budgeted
Child Care/Sitter		
Toiletries		
Cosmetics/Hair Care		
Education/Tuition		
Books/Supplies		
Child Support		
Alimony		
Subscriptions		
Organization Dues		
Gifts (inc. Christmas)		
Replace Furniture		
Pocket Money (His)		
Pocket Money (Hers)		
Baby Supplies		
Pet Supplies		
Music/Technology		
Miscellaneous		
Other _____		
Other _____		
*5-10% TOTAL		

🏃 RECREATION

	Spent	Budgeted
Entertainment		
Vacation		
5-10% TOTAL		

💰 DEBTS

	Spent	Budgeted
Car Payment 1		
Car Payment 2		
Credit Card 1 _____		
Credit Card 2 _____		
Credit Card 3 _____		
Credit Card 4 _____		
Credit Card 5 _____		
Student Loan 1		
Student Loan 2		
Student Loan 3		
Student Loan 4		
Other _____		
Other _____		
Other _____		
Other _____		
Other _____		
Your goal is 5% → 5-10% TOTAL		

Once you have completed filling out each category, subtract all category totals from your take-home pay.

Use the "income sources" form if necessary → **TAKE-HOME PAY**

Add up totals from each category → **CATEGORY TOTALS**

Remember — The goal of a zero-based budget is to get this number to zero → **ZERO BALANCE**

Financial Personality Discovery Quiz:
What's YOUR Financial Personality?

The way in which you think about, relate to, and behave with your money says a lot about your Financial Personality! Everyone's Financial Personality is different; some are more prone to save, some are more prone to spend, and others fall somewhere in-between. Being aware of what your Financial Personality is will help you to be more conscious of your tendencies when it comes to dealing with money so that you can work to avoid the pitfalls that are most commonly associated with your particular personality. Thus, discovering what your Financial Personality is can be an illuminating and fundamental step on your journey to financial empowerment!

What is your Financial Personality? Answer the questions below, and then calculate your total score to find out!

1. Which of the following *first* comes to mind when you hear the word "budget"?

    a. Restrictions

    b. Control

    c. Responsibility

    d. Time-consuming exercise

2. When you receive extra money as a work bonus, gift, etc., what do you do with it?

   a. Spend it right away

   b. Put it in the bank

   c. Daydream about what you want to buy, but you ultimately save it

   d. Spend it, but change your mind several times on what you buy

3. If you were debt-free and had $1,000 with which you could do whatever you wanted, what would you do?

   a. Spend it before it hits the bank

   b. Invest it

   c. Buy a few small things or one semi-large purchase and save the rest

   d. Buy something that's been on your wish list for a while

4. How often do you go shopping (non-grocery related)?

   a. I shop frequently

   b. I only shop out of necessity

   c. I go once or twice a month but rarely buy anything

   d. I window shop and browse online often (at least weekly) but do not always buy

5. What would you do if your car broke down today and was deemed not repairable?

   a. I need a new car anyway, so I would find my way to a dealership

   b. Withdraw some money from my savings and buy a used car with cash

   c. Think that this a terrible tragedy and can't be happening

   d. Do research to find the lowest car payment to replace it

6. When is the last time that you had $1,000 in savings?

   a. I've never really attempted to save

   b. Now

   c. Within the last year

   d. Over a year ago

Scoring

In order to calculate your Total Score…

For every "a" answer, give yourself 5 points.

For every "b" answer, give yourself 2 points.

For every "c" answer, give yourself 4 points.

For every "d" answer, give yourself 3 points.

My Total Score: _____

Results Scale

If your total score is 25-30, your Financial

Personality is:

Complete Free Spirit!

Assessment: As a Free Spirit, you go with the flow of what you want to do with your money. You are more than likely easily pulled in by the latest sales, and you spend money freely… but all is *not* lost! The toughest part for you is doing a budget, because to you, a budget feels like something is restricting you – and Free Spirits like to run with the wind, not be restricted.

Challenge: Change the way you see your budget! Rather than seeing it as a financial straitjacket that ties you down and restricts your movement, choose to see your budget as a plan that will help you get the things that you want while not jeopardizing your finances. Once you have become debt free, set aside a portion of your budget to freely spend however you like, Free Spirit!

If your total score is 19-24, your Financial Personality is: Free-spirited Nerd!

Assessment: As a Free-Spirited Nerd, you still tend to go with the flow and do what you want with your money, but you tend to analyze and think twice about making purchases that cost more than a certain amount – an amount that you have established according to your financial comfort level. Consequently, though you may take those random shopping trips to the mall, you will not spend freely; it will be capped at a certain amount, and once you reach that amount, you're done – for now. It's the little spending here and there that keeps your finances in shambles, because each of these little spending incidents add up to a large amount of money that can be a big blow to your bank account!

Challenge: The fact that you are able to restrict your spending when it approaches a certain amount says that you have a financial conscience, which allows you to exercise a moderate level of discipline over your spending. Take things a step further by developing a budget and using this same discipline to keep you operating within its limits. When you become debt free, set aside a portion of your budget to spend on as many "little things" as you like. If you want to make a purchase that costs more than what you would normally spend, save up several pay periods' worth of money that you have budgeted for the little things and use them to make whatever big purchases you like – guilt free!

If your total score is 13-18, your Financial Personality is: Nerdy Free Spirit!

Assessment: As a Nerdy Free Spirit, you like having a plan to keep your finances in order. While it is more than likely that you do not have a formal budget, the Nerd in you at least makes a half-hearted attempt to plan and regulate your spending by writing down your income and expenses on a piece of paper – or a napkin, or matchbook cover, or a sticky note – or you attempt to track your spending in your mind. However, sticking to such a non-concrete plan can be pretty tough for you, especially when the Free Spirit side of your financial personality kicks in!

Challenge: Don't kick yourself because you don't have the "formal budget thing" all together! The fact that you are making an effort to regulate your spending and that you are going through the exercise of charting your income versus your expenses for each pay period, regardless of where you might write them or how you mentally calculate them, says that you are committed to being financially responsible in your spending. As long as this is working for you – at least, for the most part – keep up the good work! You might go over in some areas of your budget, but as long as you meet your savings goals, you are good to go!

If your total score is 12, your Financial Personality is: Complete Nerd!

Assessment: As a Complete Nerd, you have probably been budgeting since you were five years old! Okay, not really, but you probably have a massive, highly-detailed Excel spreadsheet that tracks your finances for the entire year. You save naturally, and spending money is rather difficult for you. In fact, spending money for you consists of nothing more than "splurging" for sushi night at your favorite spot. Other than that, you hold on to your money and gain greater pleasure from watching the balances of your accounts rise!

Challenge: Stick to your guns, and keep up the good work! Eventually, you will become debt free and start striving towards your larger financial goals, and this will empower you to live life on a whole other level! As you enjoy, yes please spend some of your money, your life of financial empowerment, be sure to take every opportunity to educate and empower others along the way so that one day, they can live financially empowered lives just like you!

51615022R00098

Made in the USA
Columbia, SC
24 February 2019